HOW TO OPEN A RESTAURANT AND KEEP IT OPEN!

KNOWLEDGE IS THE KEY TO SUCCESS IN THE RE$TAURANT BUSINESS!

Tommy Bradburn

ISBN: 979-8-9851021-7-8

Published by Tommy Bradburn. Taos, New Mexico

Printed on acid-free paper.

DISCLAIMER

This book details the author's personal experiences with and opinions about the restaurant business.

The author and publisher are providing this book and its contents on an "as is" basis and make no representations or warranties of any kind with respect to this book or its contents. The author and publisher disclaim all such representations and warranties, including for example warranties of merchantability and expert advice for a particular purpose. In addition, the author and publisher do not represent or warrant that the information accessible via this book is accurate, complete or current.

The statements made about products and services have not been evaluated by the U.S. government. Please consult with your own legal, accounting, medical, or other licensed professional regarding the suggestions and recommendations made in this book.

Except as specifically stated in this book, neither the author or publisher, nor any authors, contributors, or other representatives will be liable for damages arising out of or in connection with the use of this book. This is a comprehensive limitation of liability that applies to all damages of any kind, including (without limitation) compensatory; direct, indirect or consequential damages; loss of data, income or profit; loss of or damage to property and claims of third parties.

You understand that this book is not intended as a substitute for consultation with a licensed medical, legal or accounting professional. Before you begin any change your lifestyle in any way, you will consult a licensed professional to ensure that you are doing what's best for your situation.

This book provides content related to restaurant topics. As such, use of this book implies your acceptance of this disclaimer.

TABLE OF CONTENTS

Introduction

This book has been written after fifty-four years of experience in the restaurant business. Its intention is to provide much-needed help to the thousands of independent restaurant operators across America. It contains a "Common Sense" approach to the restaurant business. This is not an operational manual, but rather, it's a guide to success in the restaurant business.

When you decide to open a restaurant, you do so for many reasons. One reason may be to be your own boss. Another reason is surely to make money. But if you're thinking about opening a restaurant and already in the planning stages, you could be doomed from the start. And if you're already open, but just not making it, there are reasons.

You'll find plenty of useful advice in this book. And you'll find solutions to problems you may otherwise overlook. I will talk about getting started, running the business and staying in business. I will cover such general areas as financing the restaurant, being profitable, and avoiding common pitfalls. And I will get real specific when talking about some very important procedures such as, pricing your menu, controlling your sales and losses, dealing with employees, and buying and preparing food. I will also talk a lot about attitude-----yours and your employees. So, this can be a helpful guide whether you're just beginning, heading for trouble, or already in deep trouble.

Tom C. Bradburn
July 1993

Chapter 1
Your Dream Come True

Almost since the beginning of time, the restaurant business has been around. Unfortunately, most of those restaurants are gone now. The reason: **LACK OF KNOWLEDGE!**

A MAN SAYS TO HIS WIFE, "Honey, you make the best chili! We should open a restaurant and sell it." Without any knowledge of the restaurant business, they open a restaurant to sell their chili. Three months later they're out of business. The reason: **LACK OF KNOWLEDGE!**

A man spends a couple of years managing a restaurant for a national chain. He thinks he has arrived, so he quits his job and opens his own place. After a few months he's out of business. The reason: **LACK OF KNOWLEDGE!**

Opening your own restaurant seems so easy; after all, everyone knows how to cook. Read on and you'll gain the knowledge necessary to survive this very tough business. But first here's a quick test to help you decide if this business is right for you.

Some bad points of the restaurant business:

Long hours
Dealing with the public
Strain on family life
Hundreds of problems to solve daily
Profits and sales go up and down depending on time of year
Constant employee problems

Some good points of the restaurant business:

Potential for great income
Being your own boss
Working with many different people
Meeting new friends
The glory of success---daily, weekly, monthly and yearly

If you honestly believe that the good points outweigh the bad, you may be right for the restaurant business. So now let's see what type of restaurant business is right for you

Finding a Franchise
There are many types of restaurant chains ranging from fast food to full service. There are also many ways to enter these chains. Let's examine a few ways to enter.

Each chain sells franchises. Some of the franchises are open to anyone with money. Others are closed to outsiders, and are only available to people who have spent years working with the company. You must check with individual corporate offices for details on their franchise policy.

The cheapest and most solid way to enter the world of a national restaurant chain is to get a job at one and work your way to the top. This is how I entered the world of restaurants. But again, some chains will not allow you to make it to the top or buy a franchise unless you have a great deal of money up front. So, investigate thoroughly. This method could also take you several years to achieve; however, the training you'll receive will be invaluable.

Once you have found a franchise, which will enable you to work your way to the top, get the job. Understand that this is your college. You will not get rich while you're learning, but you will get paid to learn. That is a better deal than any university in the country, since you don't get paid to go to college.

Use each day wisely. Learn all you can. Be helpful, eager and excited. Great attitudes are rewarded. Never look at where you are today, always look to the future. The pay will be low and the hours will be long, but always focus on the end result. It will be worth it.

It will take several years to learn all you need to know about this business if you apply yourself, use your time properly and pay close attention each day. Be patient. The knowledge you gain can never be taken away from you. As you learn the business, use the chapters of this book to guide you. Each section is full of the kinds of information you must learn about the chain you have chosen.

Start Your Own Chain

If you are an advanced operator, with knowledge and plenty of capitol, start your own chain. In the beginning you must decide what type of operation you would like to market and sell to others. Put together operational manuals and design the building and floor plan of the entire restaurant, including the parking lot.

After the initial legwork is done, open your first restaurant as an example for others to see. This first store must be a success. It must have moderately high volume with an attractive profit margin and should be in operation for at least one year. If you can't show strong sales and high profits, no one will want to invest in your dream.

When these things are accomplished, consult your attorney. Make sure you have an attorney who knows the legal ins and outs of putting together a franchise. When these legal steps are taken and you are ready to sell your first franchise be selective. Don't sell a franchise to just anyone. Only sell a franchise to a person or persons who will find success. You only win if they win. If they do win, maybe they will buy another, or maybe they have other "investor-type" friends would want in. The key word for you is "selective." BE SELECTIVE!

Become an Independent

Open your own restaurant and run it yourself. There are many ways to do this depending on your knowledge of the business and whether you have no cash or a lot of cash. The rest of this book is especially designed for you.

Financing

Your restaurant dream can become a reality, even if you don't have a penny to your name. You do, however, need a tremendous amount of ability, knowledge and talent in the restaurant business. If you do have that, and you can back it up with a restaurant P&L statement from a restaurant you are currently operating that has Good-Solid-Numbers, financing is very simple to find.

The first thing you should do is learn how to market yourself. Have a resume put together by a reputable company so it will have a professional look. Put this together with two years of P&L statements from the restaurant you are currently operating. This will show your ability. Remember, if you were looking to invest in a company that you knew very little about, you would look for a person with a tremendous amount of knowledge and a person who could demonstrate the ability to turn that knowledge into success. In this case, that person is YOU. Now, you should develop a plan for your restaurant. A plan consists of a concept (50's, fast food, full service, etc.), a menu, sales projections and projected profits (this can be done by using one of your old P&L's). To figure the projected sales and profits list all the expense items from your old P&L, leaving out the old numbers and plugging in your projected amounts for each expense. Subtract your expenses from your projected net sales to come up with a projected net profit.

Once again, when all of this information is complete, have a professional printer put it together for you.

Things an Investor Will Want to See

Investors are as different as you and I. Each one will look for different things in you but you can bet they will all look for opportunities to make money. They will also look for P&L statements that show a continual increase in sales and stable profits. A potential investor will also take a hard look at your controllable accounts such as, food cost; labor costs and supply cost. These are all accounts in which you (as the operator) have control over.

A prospective investor will look over your resume very carefully. They will look for stability. How long do you stay with a project? They may also look for references and follow up on them, so be accurate and thorough but make sure only to add references that will be favorable for you.

A prospective investor will also take a good look at your appearance. Any time you are meeting with a prospective investor, partner, banker or landlord you should always dress up. If you look great, you'll feel great and others will see that in you. You should always be well groomed. Remember that people will treat you the way they see you.

The conversations you have with prospective investors will probably hold the most importance. When you are asked questions, you must have logical and intelligent answers. You must also know what you are talking about and have your facts straight without sounding like you know it all. And keep in mind, this is *your* interview too. You are looking for an investor with whom you feel comfortable, and one with whom you would enjoy doing business.

You now have a professionally developed plan, resume and your past P&L's. You are dressed, properly groomed and you are somewhat educated on what a prospective investor may be looking for. The only thing you need now is a financial plan. How much money will it take? How will it be repaid? How will your prospective investor make money?

There are so many answers to all of these questions. So many, that to answer most of them, it's best if I give you an example of a deal I put together with relative ease:

I wanted to put together a restaurant, which specialized, in gourmet hamburgers. This restaurant would have inside dining, call-ins and a drive thru-window. The location was a seven on a scale of ten. The rent was to be $1250 per month for seven years. Most of the equipment that I needed for my operation were already in the building and came with the lease. All remodeling was to be done by me and at my expense.

I put a pencil to it and figured that by doing the remodeling myself but hiring an electrician and plumber to install only the necessities required to pass city code and health codes, that I could buy the remaining equipment necessary and a neon sign for outside and still have $10,000 of working capital in the bank for a $30,000 investment.

It didn't take long to find an investor. I will tell you more on how to find an investor later in this section. But for now, let me tell you that this investor had all cash. Sometimes your investor may borrow money from a bank and your restaurant may be liable for the payments on the note.

Here is what I proposed to my investor
We will form a Subchapter S Corporation (consult your attorney and accountant). I will be the president of the corporation and the investor will be the secretary. The investor will make a $30,000 loan to the corporation. The corporation will give the investor a 3 year note for the loan at current interest rates to be paid in monthly installments. In return for the loan, the investor will own 20% of the restaurant.

He agreed and I was happy to have him as a partner. He was to be a silent officer and I was to be the acting officer. We still have monthly corporate meetings to discuss our previous month's P&L statements and other business pertaining to the corporation.

You see, before I began to look for an investor, I knew all the details. I knew facts on the location of the restaurant, the cost of rent, the terms of the lease, how much cash it would take to remodel and to add all the equipment necessary to make my operation work. I also knew how I wanted to pay the loan back, over a three-year period at current interest rates with monthly payments. The restaurant would make the payments. I knew how the investor would make money. First, he would make 13% interest on the loan. Second, he would own 20% of the business, which I projected, would pay him a minimum of $1400 per month…and it did!

At the point of opening our restaurant, I became obligated to make the corporation as much profit as humanly possible. I wanted my new investor to have a very good experience with the situation for future use.

Before looking for an investor, be absolutely sure your investment package is complete: Resume, P&L statements, operation plans and financial plans. After that, finding an investor for your project can be a fairly simple matter. If you have the experience and knowledge of the restaurant business necessary, then investors are everywhere.

An investor could be your neighbor, your pastor, your landlord or a local businessperson you know. An investor is anyone who has extra cash or access to cash to invest in a safe and high return investment. An investor understands his investment is a gamble so he will check you out thoroughly. Investors must see clearly how they can make a good return on their investment.

It is not a good idea to go into business with any family members or friends. This business is simply too tough and profits margins are too fragile to have the pressures of satisfying a friend or family member.

One way to find investors is by word of mouth. Tell people who have plenty of cash that you are looking for an investor. Another way to find an investor is to place an ad in your local newspaper. A simple example is:

Investor needed
Local restaurant venture
Contact Tom at: 555-9310

Run this ad for one week and wait for your phone to ring, and it will. Investors are curious by nature.

When your phone does ring, be relaxed. Briefly explain your plan. Let them know that you have P&L statements, a resume and a financial plan. DO NOT MENTION THE AMOUNT YOU NEED OVER THE PHONE! Instead, set up a meeting. Give your program a chance. This calls for a face-to-face meeting. A nice restaurant is a great place to discuss your program with your potential investor. Again, keep in mind that this is *your* interview also. You are looking for an investor with whom you will be happy doing business. If you sign up the wrong investor you could create more problems for yourself that you ever imagined. BE SELECTIVE!

If you hold several interviews with no success, you may consider running your ad for another week. You may also consider running your ad in another newspaper, perhaps one in another larger town close to you. DON'T GIVE UP!

Once you have a commitment from an investor, you have much to do before you actually receive any money. You must pay a visit to your attorney to determine what type of agreement you want to work out. You and your investor could simply form a partnership. That is a simple, cheap and painless process for you both. A Subchapter S Corporation is a bit more complicated and more expensive, but offers you and your investor more protection and tax advantages. At this point you may also want the advice of your accountant.

Your attorney will also need to draw up a note to the investor. If you form a corporation, a corporate resolution will be necessary in order for you to open a checking account in the name of the corporation. Your attorney will take care of everything. Attorney fees (for corporations) can cost anywhere from $1000 to $2000 depending on your needs. Partnership agreements will cost from $200 to $400. Let your attorney and accountant make this decision for you as they will have your best interest at heart. An LLC may also be a good way to go. Explain to your attorney and accountant what it is that you are trying to accomplish and they will point you in the right direction.

After the papers are drawn up, you and your investor will meet at your attorney's office to sign the paperwork. At this time, your investor will hand you a check for is investment. You will be required to take this check to your bank and open a checking account in the name of your company.

Conventional Financing

Banks do not generally like to loan money for restaurant equipment. They recognize how risky the business is. The bank may only loan 70% or 80% of what you need. They may also require you to put up some additional collateral.

With good credit, a bank is a great way to go. This will allow you to own 100% of your restaurant. However, the investor is generally a wise person who has a great deal of common sense to help you solve some of the tough problems that you face. An investor's advice at a corporate meeting may be just what you need to keep your operation smooth, organized and profitable.

No Credit? No Problem.

There are thousands of restaurants that have gone out of business that are easy to lease and are already full of equipment. Owners of these closed restaurants are usually eager to lease. So, the only expense you will have are your sign, painting, cleaning, permits and utility deposits. Never open a restaurant where one has just closed until you have made drastic visual changes outside. This tells your customers that something new is replacing the old. The more outside work that you do, and the longer you take with it, the better. The restaurant before you may have had a bad reputation or some other negative stigma attached to it, which caused it to close. You job is to first overcome this with as much inexpensive visual change as possible.

Restaurant Investing

Be an Investor

If you want to be a restaurant investor, you must find an experienced and stable "restaurant person" to be your restaurant manager. Make sure it's someone you can trust and someone with whom you'd like to be in business. You may already know someone. If not, run an ad in your local newspaper and conduct interviews. In order to make it worthwhile for him, you may want to pay this person a "manager's salary" of $350-$400 per week, plus a percentage of profits. Maybe 10% of the profits the first year, 15% the second year, 20% the third year, etc. Don't be greedy. Remember that the person running the operation is the person who can make or break it.

Find an Investor

If you are a smooth and profitable restaurant operator who is going nowhere, find an investor. Get your Profit and Loss (P&L) statements together. Two years of P&L's show stability and a comparison of one year to the next. Maybe you know someone with money that would like to invest. If not, put an ad in your newspaper or several different newspapers and conduct interviews to find the right investor for you.

Before you put an ad in the newspaper, you need to know what you want from an investor. I would shoot for an 80/20 partnership, with the investor supplying the money and you supplying the hard work and sweat.

Chapter 2
Getting Your Restaurant Off the Ground

Pre-Opening

The financing is complete. All the papers are signed, including your lease agreement. Now it is time to get to work…and I mean WORK. The period of time from signing your lease to opening your restaurant will be the busiest period of time you have ever experienced.

It's very important to give your restaurant a professional look. Some customers and friends will say to you that they had rather spend their money at locally-owned restaurants than at a franchise or corporate restaurant. You are in a unique position to give your restaurant a corporate look and to also be locally owned. You can enjoy the best of both worlds.

It doesn't cost a lot to look professional, but it does take planning. It's a good idea to have your restaurant's name on your main sign out front and also on your building. This visually ties the two together. Put your name on everything possible--- your drive-thru menu board, your menus themselves and any printing you have done.

If you have to open without printed cups, sacks, napkins, etc., it is important to buy cups with some type of design on them.

Don't buy plain white cups. Plain cups mean to the customer that you are nobody. Over a period of time, these imprinted cups will become a signature of yours. Later you may want to investigate the possibility of having your name and logo imprinted on your cups.

Floor Plan

Whether you open a full-service restaurant or a fast-food restaurant, the work areas for your employees must be laid out with timesaving and step-saving efficiency in mind.

During lunch, customers are generally in a hurry and it is very important that your kitchen equipment – drink machine, ice machine, etc. – are placed in your work areas in a way that allows your employees to fill each order with efficiency and speed. For example, it would be very time consuming for an employee to get ice for a drink in one location and have to take a few steps to get to the drink machine for a soft drink.

If you have no experience at setting up a restaurant, have a restaurant equipment company help you with this. A company trained in these areas can be very helpful.

Before any work begins on your restaurant, you must report to your city building inspector and county health department. Depending on the amount of remodeling to be done, they may require a drawing of your plans. You can usually do this drawing yourself, by using a ruler and typing paper to make your drawings to some type of scale. These City inspectors will then usually come to your location to see what your plan looks like in person.

When you are approved, you may begin work. When your work is complete, simply give them a call for a final inspection. They will then come back to your location for the inspection. You must then take this inspection report to City Hall for your certificate of occupancy.

This procedure will vary from city to city. Each city has its own standards, procedures and methods. It's important to understand that these inspectors are on your side. Sometimes they may seem unreasonable to you, but their job is to see that you have the opportunity to operate in a safe and healthy building. Work with them and they will work with you.

Signs and Logos
The very beginning of your remodeling is the time to call your sign company and order your sign. This could take four to six weeks, so you must get this process started early. If you do not have a logo or a fantastic idea for your sign, these people are very creative and will be a great deal of help to you. What you want, in a sign, is one which is simple, easy to read; easy to see from a distance and one which is cheerful and inviting. Remember; strive for that professional, franchise look.

Uniforms
Now is the time to decide on the type of uniforms you want your employees to wear. If these need to be ordered, they will need to

be ordered early in your program. A money-saving word of advice: Only order large uniform tops. Otherwise, you will have money tied up in a uniform that on one can wear. Even the smallest employee will look fine in a large top.

Insurance

At this point, you should also call your insurance company. Your landlord will spell out in your lease the amount of coverage for his building. Yes, you will be required to place insurance on his building. You will also need to insure the contents. Most states, but not all, also require you to carry workman's comp. Insurance. The rate for workman's comp. is set by the state in which you operate. Your insurance representative will have all those facts.

Competition

As your pre-opening work progresses, you'll find that you are probably eating out more often. Use this time to check out the competition. Competition is any establishment that sells food in your area. Check out the appearance of the restaurant. Is it clean and well-kept? Did you notice the sign as you approached the parking lot? Is the dining room neat and clean? How's the atmosphere? How do the employee's look? Most important of all, how are the employee's attitudes? How long did you have to wait to place your order? How long did you have to wait to receive your order? How was the appearance of the food? How was the taste of the food? How were the prices?

These are the people you are competing with. Continue this process throughout your entire pre-opening program. When you open, you'll know who your real competition is. Try to be very objective and honest as you evaluate these other restaurants.

Vendors

As your project nears completion, it's time for you to deal with two other very important matters---choosing your food and supply vendors and hiring your crew.

Being an independent operator means you will pay very high prices for your food and supplies. After you are open for a year and your sales increase, your prices will begin to come down. The price you pay for food and supplies will constantly need to be monitored by you. Many suppliers will raise their prices once they have your business. You must be aware of this and not allow that to happen. You may even want to mention to your salesperson that you will not tolerate a company who quotes low prices in the beginning only to raise them later.

All the franchise restaurants either have their own commissary which sets prices, or they may use the same suppliers that you do with prices which are locked in. As an independent, you must monitor your prices each time you order. One way for an independent to keep his prices in line and stable is to use two different suppliers. It is a bit more complicated to deal with two suppliers, as you will have different salespeople, twice as many deliveries and have to write twice as many checks. But this double work can be worth it to you; because these companies will be more competitive knowing that they could lose your business to another company if they are not careful and fair. I do not recommend using two suppliers unless your supplier is unreasonable, at which time you may want to change altogether.

It is important to know that these salespeople make their living by selling…by selling to you.

The day before you place your initial order, you should sit down with your menu in front of you and make a list of every ingredient you will need to prepare each item.
An example is:

Ham and cheese sandwich = Ham, Bread, Mayonnaise, lettuce, tomato, cheese, and pickles

You will also need to include any items necessary to package the sandwich whether the order is to "eat here" or "to go".

Ham and cheese sandwich = salt & pepper shakers, salt & pepper packets, bottled ketchup, ketchup packets, sandwich bags or tissue paper for wrapping, to go sacks, napkins.

Through this process you will get all the items necessary to prepare the product whether the customer eats at the restaurant or takes it with them. You will want to make sure you are very thorough with this list so you don't miss anything. Now is the time to really "pick your brain" so that your initial food and supply orders are complete.

When you have a complete list of food and supplies, you must turn to cleaning and bathroom supplies. Don't forget hand towel and soap dispensers. The larger suppliers will sell paper towels, soap and toilet paper dispensers for 1 cent as long as you buy their supplies. Most large suppliers also have available (at no charge to you) coffee machines, tea dispensers and jet spray machines for specialty drinks such as punch, lemonade, etc. Ask your salesperson for details.

As stated before, your salesperson is very good at selling. With this initial order, they will remind you of many things you might have forgotten. Do not, however, let this person sell you things you don't need. They are also very good at that.

How much should I buy? I cannot answer that question without knowing more about the type of restaurant you are opening, your location, the area you are in and your pre-opening advertising. You must, however, be prepared. Ordering too little at this point could be disastrous. You will need to work very closely with all of your salespeople.

If you are in a city of 50,000 or more, your supply companies will normally have trucks delivering every day. This can be helpful for you and your salesperson. Your salesperson knows the market area better than you and can be particularly helpful. Make sure you have your salesperson's home number. If you run short of any item after opening, your salesperson should be able to help you day or night. That's their job. If it turns out that you over-ordered a perishable item, your salesperson should be able to replace it or you can return it.

Chapter 3
Your Crew

This will be the most difficult area you will have to deal with throughout your restaurant career. There are however, several things you can do as an independent to eliminate many of the problems other restaurants face every day.

1. Learn how to hire. Don't hire someone just because you need help. Hold out for that person who will fit in with you and your crew's way of thinking, work habits, appearance and attitudes. If you are short-handed, you never win by hiring someone just to fill a need. You only win by being very selective and patient.

2. Most independent restaurants don't make it because they don't give a second thought to attitude. It is critical to have a happy-go-lucky attitude throughout your store, while still maintaining professional work habits.

To foster the right attitude in your employees, start during the hiring process by giving a little speech which should go something like this: "Despite the fact that I will train you and direct you during the period of time you work here; I will not be your boss? Your boss will always be each and every customer who comes into our restaurant. If you do a great job with our customers by being friendly, cheerful and professional, and if you make sure their order is always correct and prepared to perfection, and if you do all you can to make sure their experience with us is the absolute best possible, we will all get a raise, because we will have more customers every day. But if you do not do these things, all of our jobs could be in jeopardy because our customers will choose to eat someplace else. Our customers have the power to fire everyone here, including the owner, by choosing to eat someplace else.

We must understand that our customers do not have to eat here! They have many other choices. Our job is to ALWAYS do more than our part to make sure our customers always want to eat at our restaurant.

3. Keep your own attitude positive at all times. You set the example.

4. A busy crew is a happy crew. When employees have too much time to gossip; trouble is sure to follow.

5. Have a list of employee rules. As soon as you hire an employee you should give them a copy to take home with them.

Here is an example:

EMPLOYEE RULES

1. Our customers will always come before any other duties
2. Never be late for work
3. No visitors while on duty
4. No phone calls while on duty
5. No gum chewing while on duty
6. If you need a day off; management must be notified at least 1 week in advance
7. Uniforms must always be worn properly
8. Long hair must be tied back
9. Men must be clean shaven

You should make your own list of things which are important to you. You can also add to this list as problems arise in the future. This list of rules is designed to cut down on nonsense and also as a form of communication.

6. No matter how small your company is, communication will always be a vital part of your success. A monthly employee meeting is always a great way to communicate with your crew. These meetings should always be positive and supportive in nature.

Monthly meetings are a time to inform your crew of things going on now, or of things coming up in the future such as specials, promotions or special events. Select an employee of the month. Give that employee twenty-five dollars for his or her outstanding performance. Put his or her name on a plaque or on your marquee for a few days. This is a great motivation builder. Have frequent contests for your crew.

Example;

Have some coupons printed up with a particular item that you want to promote in your restaurant, such as, a "Buy one get one free ham sandwich". Have your crew sign the backs of these coupons and pass them out to people, away from your restaurant. The employee who has the most coupons redeemed by a customer during the month wins $50, or whatever amount you feel is appropriate.

You may want to put a chart on a wall in a work area to keep a running tally of how many coupons each employee received each day. Your crew will love this and your promotion will be a huge success. Have the awards ceremony at you next employee meeting.

7. Operate your restaurant in a professional and businesslike manner. Your crew will respect you for it and your business will grow. If you have a dining room, don't sit out front and chat with everyone who comes along. Work as hard as your crew, or harder. Set high standards, your customers will appreciate it.

8. Evaluate your staffing needs carefully and hire accordingly. Again, I cannot say how many employees you will need to open your restaurant. You certainly do not want to be understaffed. But many of the people you hire will not make it through the first week. Several may not survive the first day. You must anticipate high sales the first week or so whether you have them or not. If your sales are high and you don't have the crew you need to take care of it, you will not have high sales very long.

Remember; an opening is a very special time for you and your customers. With that in mind, you should have three full crews plus two or three extra employees for each crew.

Example;

Crew One: Full day drew plus 2 or 3. This crew will normally work Monday through Friday and are off on Saturday and Sunday

Crew TWO: Full night crew plus 2 or 3. This crew may work three nights and then work days on Saturday and Sunday

Crew Three: Full night crew plus 2 or 3. This crew will work four nights.

This is how I would organize my opening crews. Yes, it seems heavy; however, you have no idea how busy your opening will be. You have spent a great deal of money up to this point and you must protect that investment. If sales taper off, as they usually do after a couple of weeks, you should begin to trim these crews back a little.

9. Keep schedules organized and stay on top of all the paperwork. When you hire an employee, he or she must fill out an application which you must keep on file. He or she must also fill out a W4 form which you will send to your accountant. As you hire your opening crew, you must determine who will make up your day crew and who will make up your alternating night crews. Design a simple work schedule and have a print shop print at least twenty copies of it. As you hire an employee, write his or her name in the proper space with the hours he or she will work. See example;

Date							
DAY SHIFT							
	Mon.	**Tues.**	**Wed.**	**Thurs.**	**Fri.**	**Sat.**	**Sun.**
Jane	10- 1	10- 1	10- 1	10- 1	10- 1	OFF	10- 1
Brian	11- 5	11- 5	11- 5	11- 5	OFF	11- 5	9- 5
Mary	11- 2	11- 2	11- 2	OFF	11- 2	OFF	11- 2
Ray	9- 5	9- 5	9- 5	9- 5	9- 5	9- 5	OFF
NIGHT SHIFT							
Bill	5- 10	5- 10	5- 10	OFF	5- 10	OFF	5- 10
Steve	6- 9	OFF	6- 9	OFF	6- 9	OFF	6- 9
Jay	OFF	OFF	OFF	5- 10	OFF	5- 10	OFF
Bob	OFF	5- 10	OFF	5- 10	5- 10	5- 10	OFF

Comments

After you've completed all the physical work of setting up the restaurant, it's time to call the city for your final inspection. After this inspection and approval, you can get your Certificate of Occupancy for City Hall. With this Certificate you are free to open. This is a great time to have your first employee meeting.

During this meeting you will acquaint the employees with their work areas, explain how the operation works and motivate them to work together as a team.

Take all of your cashiers, for instance, to their work area and explain their duties and responsibilities. Walk through the entire order-taking process with them. Stress the importance of a smile and greeting the customers with a "Hi, how are you doing today?" Make sure they also understand the importance of being polite, courteous and helpful.

Use the same procedure with your kitchen staff. Stress quality and perfection. Only sell the best product possible. Explain to your cooks that even though they may not have direct contact with the customer, they should put a smile in the food they cook. Explain to them how critical their job is to your operation.

One More Thing before Opening Day
It's always a great idea before opening to have what is called a "dry run". This means that you get your entire crew together to cook some free food for a group of people such as your police department or school teachers. Have your crew in their

designated positions and have your group order as a customer normally would. Have the cashier take the order just like a normal situation. If you have a major problem during this practice run you may want to have another one. Don't open until you are confident with your crew. This enables you to test your operation and gives your crew a chance to see how your operation works with customers. It also gives you the opportunity to solve any equipment problems, employee problems or operational problems before you actually open.

Chapter 4
Opening Day

Your dream is coming true today. Excitement is running high. Smiles and pride are everywhere. Your crew looks great in their new uniforms and your restaurant looks even better. On this day you must realize you are the organizer. You must organize the food preparation, your employees' work schedules, food deliveries such as bread, milk, produce and so on; you must organize the entire operation and that can be an overwhelming day indeed.

Customer service and quality of food must be at an all-time high today. Understand that on the average, each customer you serve today will talk to thirteen other people about you, your menu and your service. It is the job of you and your crew to make sure the news your first costumers spread about you and your restaurant is always good news. I don't want to say it's a "make or break" day, but it is a very critical day for your future. This day is the main reason you need extra crew members, to have the time necessary to check with customers and to make sure that everything is all right and to solve problems which may arise.

For an independent it is less risky to open slowly. You don't have trained crew members with you who know how to solve problems and insure a smooth and professional operation. From a slow start, word-of-mouth about your great food and excellent, friendly service will spread. That's how sales grow each day. This concept would be less risky than being over-run with customers who you can't possibly care for properly. Slow is the approach I would recommend. Little to no advertising. Pass out a few-hundred flyers in your immediate area a couple of hours before you open to insure some kind of crowd. If you and your crew handle this well, then tomorrow will be a better day and the next day will be even better. This will allow you and your crew time to work out the kinks and establish a workable routine before the store gets really busy.

After you've been open for a week or so your crew should be coming along nicely. If so, you may consider having a "Grand Opening" to persuade more new customers to give you a try. You can accomplish this by having several outrageous specials—maybe a costumed character, or any other special event you may dream up.

This is a time for your crew to look great and to perform at their highest level. A Grand Opening should have a carnival-like atmosphere. Everyone should have fun, including YOU! Grand Opening day is when most rules go out the door and few profits are made. Today is an investment in all of your tomorrows. Plan your Grand Opening carefully. Have plenty of crew working on this day.

I keep saying that great food and great service are the keys to success in the restaurant business, and it's true. Every restaurant owner thinks they have great food and service. But let's investigate further and shed some light on what constitutes great food and great service.

As far as great food is concerned, your food must be cooked properly without taking short cuts. Your food must be HOT, fresh and great-looking. The appearance of your food is a big part of what puts in it the great category.

Great service means different things to different people, but the key to great service is being consistent. A great attitude and enthusiasm seem to be difficult to find these days, but they can certainly make the difference in how your restaurant runs.

Here's an example of how attitude and enthusiasm can play a role in your operation.

If you have a drive-thru window, instruct your employees to speak plainly and slowly. Your customers will truly appreciate being able to hear and understand each word the drive-thru crewperson speaks. Also instruct your employees to press the talk button until they are finished with all they are saying. This is an industry-wide problem. Employees begin talking a second or two before they press the talk button. And to add insult to injury, many people release the button a second or two before they finish speaking. Get this running smoothly and you won't believe the number of positive comments you'll receive from your customers.

At the drive-thru always greet your customers with a bounce in your voice. "Hi, welcome to Mel's. May I take your order please?" Always listen to every word your customer is saying. Asking customers to repeat their order makes them feel like you were not paying attention. Always pay close attention! When the customer has finished giving the order, you should repeat it back to him or her slowly so every word can be heard, then ask cheerfully, "Will there be anything else?" If not, give your customer the total price and ask them to drive thru. As your customer reaches the window, greet them with eye contact and a great smile. Be very cheerful and helpful at the window. As customers pay and you give them their change, be friendly and ask if they would like salt or ketchup with their order. If not, tell them their order will be right out. When their order is complete, hand it to them, make eye contact again, and say, "Thank you. You have a fantastic day." I'm telling you from forty years of experience that customers are not used to that type of enthusiastic treatment and will return to your restaurant again and again just to see if you are still as excited.

Inside should have the same excitement. Make eye contact and smile as the customer approaches the counter. As soon as they are close enough, greet the customer enthusiastically. Ask, "How are you today?" and then ask, "What can I do for you today?" If they have trouble deciding, you may want to make a recommendation or suggestion. For example:

"Ma'am or sir, do you like mushrooms? If you do, we have a grilled mushroom burger that's fantastic with a little Swiss cheese on it." With a suggestion like that, your customers will have a mushroom burger with Swiss, nine times out of ten.

Or…"We have fantastic catfish fillets with fries, hush puppies and some of the best slaw this side of the Mississippi." And with that recommendation, guess what they'll have for lunch?

After customers have received their meals and gotten situated, a crewmember should stop by to see if everything is O.K., or if they need anything else. Later, nearing the end of the meal, stop by for drink refills. Always use that great smile and cheerful voice. As the customers are leaving, be sure to invite them back and don't forget to say, "Have a fantastic day."

It's the attitude and enthusiasm, which are different here. Anyone can sell food, but not everyone can dish out the kind of winning attitude your crew should have. My restaurants have received many letters from customers over the years. They're almost always the same. Here is an excerpt from one of those letters.

"I have eaten at every restaurant in this town. After I gave yours a try, I was in shock, to say the least. Your crew greeted me, as I entered your building, asked if everything was all right during my meal, invited me to have a free refill, thanked me and asked me to return as I was leaving. But the most astonishing part was what took place outside when we were leaving. One of your employees was apparently on break. He looked up at us, smiled and said, "Thanks for stopping by." You guys had better watch

it. If word gets out about your great food and astonishing service, there might be a stampede to your restaurant. Keep up the great job!"

If you think enthusiasm and caring about your customers are not important, you are mistaken. It works like magic. Nothing in your business life should matter more to you than your customers, and it certainly doesn't hurt to show it.

So now that we've gotten through the pre-opening, it's time to look forward to that first day in business. The anticipation is over and tomorrow will be the most hectic day you have ever seen. But now you are a new restaurant owner. Congratulations!

Now you know the basics of opening a restaurant. Well, opening up is the easy part. It is much easier to open a restaurant, than it is to keep a restaurant open. This is one of the most demanding businesses I know of. It is stressful and tiring.

If it sounds as if I am trying to scare you off, I'm not. I'm just being honest. But despite all the pressures, the restaurant business can also be fun and rewarding.

Someone once asked me to briefly tell them what it is like to be an owner/operator of a restaurant. I thought for a minute and so many things came to mind. I couldn't explain it briefly. I went home that evening and thought about that question, and then it came to me.

Being a restaurant owner/operator is like being a single parent. In the beginning it will take every ounce of your time, attention and energy. You will get very little sleep. You think about it all the time and if your business hurts, you hurt. If it screams out, you must be there for it. There will be many days it will need extra special attention all day and all night. It will be all consuming for the first year or two.

You must feed, clothe and nurture it, and then it will begin to grow. As it grows, it will need less constant attention, but it will always need to be watched closely so that it won't go astray.

You will always feel very proud of it, even during the darkest hours. As it matures, you can begin to step back and watch it with pride. You will reminisce about all that you have been through together and all you have accomplished. There's not another feeling like it.

Chapter 5
Help with some common mistakes

The real purpose of this book is to help the independent restaurant operator. Some of you are already in deep trouble, some are headed for trouble and some are beginning your dream. Through no fault of your own, except lack of knowledge, many independents make critical mistakes which lead to financial problems in a hurry. In this chapter we will try to address these critical mistakes and give you some help immediately.

Location

I overheard a very successful restaurant owner say that the three most important factors in the restaurant business are location, location and location.

I do agree that location is very important. In fact, one hundred yards could cost you thousands of dollars in sales and profits. For instance, let's say you find a building and parking lot that is perfect for you and this location is on the busiest street in town, but the rent is $2500 per month. Then you notice there is another site around the corner, which also fits your needs, and the rent is only $1850 per month. Wow! That's a savings of $7800 per year. You may be really excited about this less expensive location, but by being on a side street instead of the main street could cost you up to $100,000 or $200,000 per year in sales.

These lost sales could translate into \$20,000 to \$40,000 in profits. Investigate both sites thoroughly.

The second part of location is need. Is there really a need for your restaurant in a particular area? For instance, are there more customers in the area than restaurants? Is every restaurant in the area completely full every day at lunch? Are they all excessively busy in the morning hours before noon and are they busy for a couple of hours after noon? How's the night business? Are all the restaurants extremely busy? If so, there may be a need for you to relieve the pressure from them. If not, you've moved into an area with very stiff competition. If you're an experienced operator, this may not matter. If you're a first-time restaurant operator, you may find the going tough.

Areas, which have a need for a restaurant, may be around a large hospital with little to no competition. An area, around several factories, with little to no competition may be good for you. Another good possibility may be at an intersection of two major highways. Just remember to always ask the question, is there really a need for my restaurant in this area?

Sometimes, which side of the street you're on can make a tremendous difference. Are the restaurants on one side of the street busier than the restaurants on the other side? Why do you think that is? It could be that access might be easier on one side of the street than the other.

Maybe much of the traffic on this street is people who live out of town. When they're coming into town, it's early in the morning. These people may be looking for a quick breakfast. If breakfast is your thing, your restaurant may need to be on this side of the street. After work, the side of the street leading out of town may be the most productive for restaurants. Check this out over a several day period.

If you're already in operation and just not doing well because of your location, there is still hope for you. There are two possible solutions. Before we get into those, we must first make absolutely sure the location is the problem and not the operation.

For instance, was there a time when your restaurant experienced high sales but now the sales are low? If so, there could be a problem with your operation. You may need to go back and reread the section on "Running your business".

Or, let's say that your restaurant has never been busy since opening day. It could be that you are in a good location, bur that you are not taking advantage of the location. Take a good look at your restaurant from across the street during the daylight hours and at night. Ask these questions: Does my restaurant look open? If not, what could I do to make it look open? Is my restaurant well lit? Again, does it look open at night? Is your sign adequate? Does your restaurant look inviting?

You see, if you answer "no" to any of these questions, then you could probably make better use of your present location. But, if you can honestly answer "yes" to all of the previous questions, then the problem could very well be location.

Two Possible Solutions

1. If your sales are weak but not disastrous, you might be able to renegotiate your rent payments. Go to your landlord and tell him your sales are a little weak and that they have been since opening day. Tell him that with a little time that you can increase your sales. Maybe you could ask for a rent reduction for six months or a year while you work on your sales. You may be surprised by your landlord's answer. He may respect you for being straightforward and he may not want to go through the hassle of finding a new tenant. He may just say OK. It doesn't hurt to ask. Ask and you shall receive. It could put an extra $1000 per month in your pocket.

2. If rent reductions won't make a difference, or if your landlord says no, you may consider moving to another location, now that you know what to look for in a location. In this situation, I'm assuming that you're on a month-to-month lease with no long-term obligation to your present landlord. Moving is expensive and you may not have the cash. Maybe you need an investor to help you. Look under "Financing" in this book to learn how to gain the cash you may need for a move.

I would suggest moving only as a last resort. If you're convinced that you know how to operate a restaurant properly, but in the beginning you made a terrible mistake with your location selection; a move may be the answer. If you're a good operator, and you've used all your sales-building ability, but you just can't win, it's better to move on than to go down with a sinking ship.

Menu Selection and Pricing

Many independents have more menu than they need. Being efficient in the restaurant business is very important. It's difficult to be efficient or fast with an expanded menu. Both of these should be a concern of yours. A large menu will cause you to order, store, inventory and pay for more food than is necessary. It also makes it more complicated to train your crew because everyone has much more to learn. A better method may be to specialize in something, maybe hot dogs, hamburgers or spaghetti. Then add a few simple side items. Now you have a simple menu, which is streamlined and efficient. With this menu you need less storage and have less money tied up in inventory which means higher profits. Later, after you've been open for a while and your crew is trained, you can add new menu items as sales builders if necessary.

Being an independent, you can't afford to have items on your menu that don't sell. If you do, all your money will be tied up in inventory. If you have a slow-moving item on your menu, monitor the sales of that item for an entire week. If this item is one percent or less of your total sales you might consider taking it off your menu. THIS ITEM IS COSTING YOU MONEY!

An example could be salads. If you have salads on your menu and they don't sell, for one reason or other, they must go. What are the items you can trim from your inventory because of this item? You could eliminate the containers you package them with. You could get rid of your dressings, croutons, bacon bits, crackers, etc. Now you have drastically reduced your inventory and added this money to your profits where it belongs. Keep your menu lean, mean and simple.

Menu Pricing

Most restaurants operate on food costs ranging from 29 to 38 percent depending on the type of restaurant you decide to open. This means that 29 to 38 cents of every dollar in sales will be spent for the purchase of your food. So, the pricing of your menu could be the most critical part of your operation. Many new restaurants don't make it because their menu items are underpriced or overpriced.

Fast food restaurants have lower food cost that a steak house. The steak house is dealing with higher-priced menu items than a fast-food restaurant. For instance, a meal at a steak house may cost the customer $15. A 10% profit on this meal would be $1.50. At a fast-food restaurant, a meal might cost $3.40. A 10% profit on this meal would only be 34 cents.

You can quickly recognize that a fast-food restaurant must operate with a higher percentage of profit than 10%. Usually, they must make over 20% to do well. The steak house can often times operate well on a 15% net profit, depending on sales.

Food cost percentage should be determined by your ticket average. To compute your ticket average, divide your net sales for the day by the number of customers for the day. (Net sales are your sales minus sales tax)

EXAMPLE: $1857.65 SALES divided by 451 customers = $4.12

My recommendations would be:
Ticket average of $5 or less = 31% food cost
Ticket average of $5 to $8 = 33% food cost
Ticket average over $10 = 35% food cost

These are only examples and should not be etched in stone; however, I believe these will be a good guide for you to follow.

For the independent, it is difficult to compete with the prices of a national chain. The chain buys in such large quantities that the prices they pay for food will be much lower than the price you will pay. One example would be the price of a five-gallon tank of cola. A national may pay $29 per tank, while you may pay $36 or more for the exact same product. If you try to compete with the national boys on price, you're making a terrible mistake.

What your customer will demand from you is for the price to be fair for what they receive. So, to justify a higher price, your product must either be perceived as a real value for the money or an outstanding and unusual product.

Let me say this, if the attitudes of you and your crew are well above average, and your food is really something to be proud of, the price will be less of a concern to your customers.

It could take up to six months before you know if you have priced your menus properly. The national boys already have their pricing taken care of because they have so many restaurants and so much experience.

With the independent, it's been hit or miss, which is a terrible way to survive in this extremely tough business. I can get you very close, but I feel that you will need to make some small adjustments by your sixth month.

In the restaurant business, some of your menu items will need to maintain a very high food cost and others a very low food cost. For instance, soft drinks and fries will carry a very low food cost and this will help you to hold the line on your higher food cost items, such as steak, hamburgers, etc.

Computing your menu prices is the most tedious and time-consuming process in the restaurant business, and it's also one of the most important. The time-consuming part of this process is determining the cost of your product. What does it cost you to make this item? When you know the answer to that question, you can begin to solve many of your problems. This process is long and boring, but critical to the financial stability of your restaurant.

Let's begin with a simple item, such as French fries. Frozen fries normally will come to you in six; 4-pound bags (24 lb. Total). Open a bag of your fries and portion them out as you normally would for an order so that you can find out how many orders you will actually sell from a bag. An order of fries is normally four ounces. Let's say you were able to get 15 orders of fries out of each bag. Now determine the actual cost of a bag of fries.

Let's say a case of fries costs you $14.75 and there are six bags per case. Divide $14.75 by 6. ($14.75/6 = $2.46. Your cost for each bag of fries is $2.46. To determine the cost per order, divide $2.46 by 15 (the number of orders you get from each bag. ($2.46/15 = .164). So, it costs you 16.4 cents per order of fries. Now, before you jump up and down because of this low price, don't forget to add the cost of your shortening. When working up the food costs of any item, you must figure the cost of each food item used to prepare the product.

Normally, you'll find it possible to cook approximately 300 orders of fries with 35 pounds of shortening before your shortening needs changing. Let's say that your shortening costs $13 for 35 pounds. To determine your cost for shortening (per order) simply divide $13 by 300 orders ($13/300 = .043). This is approximately one-half cent. So, add .05 cents for the shortening to 16.4 cents for the fries (.05 + 16.4 = 16.9). Your total cost to produce an order of fries is 16.9 cents. To compute the price, you should charge for this order of fries, you must first determine what percentage of sales you feel you should pay for food. In other words, what do you feel your food cost percentage should be? Remember:

Ticket average of $5 or less = 31% food cost
Ticket average of $5 to $8 = 33% food cost
Ticket average over $10 = 35% food cost

Let's say that you decide that 32% is realistic for you. Divide 100 by 32. (100/32 = 3.125). Round it off to 3.13. Now multiply the cost of the item (fries = 16.9 cents) by 3.13. (16.9 x 3.13 = 52.897) So, for a 32% food cost, you should charge 53 cents per order for fries. But you have to allow for waste and you should charge more for fries so that you can charge less for higher-priced items that cost you more, such as burgers and steaks. In other words, with items such as fries, you should charge as much as the market will bear. Use the fact that you can charge more than 53 cents for fries, to compensate for charging less on your more expensive items. I'm not saying to charge the same price as everyone else, please NEVER do that. If you charge the same price for a steak as your competition, just because that's what they charge, I'd say that's very foolish and the kind of logic that puts many independents out of business. You see, you have no idea what your competitor paid for his steak; you only know what you have paid. You must charge a price based on what you pay for your food, or you're doomed before you even open.

Please understand, this is a process that most independents do not go through. I understand why. It's confusing, lengthy and a whole lot of trouble, but if you are to survive in this business, you must learn this process. If you just cannot understand it, find a very bright math student from a high school or a math teacher for help. Or go to a local college math department for help, but never open a restaurant until you have gone through this entire process with every food item on your menu. If you bypass this very critical step, you may find no money left for you at the end of each month. in fact, you could end each month further and further in debt.

Let's run through the formula one more time because it's so very important. Determine your actual cost of the product. Determine what you want your food cost percentage to be (normally between 29% and 38% depending on the type of restaurant you open). Divide 100 by your determined food cost. Multiply this by the actual cost of the product.

This is the price you should charge for each item on your menu; however, remember that you will have items such as soft drinks and fries with very low food costs and other items with very high food costs. Let's say and 8 oz. Rib eye costs you $2.99 per pound. If so, each rib eye will cost you $1.50. If you decide that you want your food cost on each steak to be 35%, then divide 100 by 35. You'll get 2.86. Multiply 2.86 by $1.50, which is $4.29.

Can you charge $4.29 for the steak alone? Maybe. Maybe not. You could offset this price by putting a meal together: an 8-oz. Rib eye, a baked potato and a roll. You already know that the rib eye cost you $1.50. Now, figure the cost of the potato and the roll. Let's say you come up with 23 cents per potato and 10 cents per roll. So, your total cost for the meal is $1.83. With a food cost of 35% on this meal, (100/35 = 2.86) (2.86 x 1.83 = $5.23), you can charge $5.23 for a rib eye steak, a baked potato and a roll. This will make more sense to your customers than $4.29 for a lonely steak. It's the baked potato, which brought the high cost of your steak into a realistic price for you customer.

Learning how to compute food cost on each item will be a very important tool for you to use throughout your restaurant career. A tool most independents do not use. You'll have an edge and will be able to more closely predict your success. Leave the guesswork to others; you become a professional with deliberate actions.

When To Increase Prices

It's difficult to say exactly when you should have a price increase, but as the price you pay for food continues to rise, you must eventually offset those higher costs.

Let's say that over a three-month period, your food cost percentage has risen from 31.5% to 32.5%. Is it time for a price increase? Maybe not. You must look at all the variables.

Are produce prices temporarily skyrocketing? That happens every few years, but these prices will eventually come down, so most experienced restaurant owners do not become alarmed by this type of temporary situation. This would not be a justifiable reason for a price increase since the situation is only a temporary problem.

Here are four other areas to look if there is no obvious reason why your food cost percentage has increased. These are all areas you can control if you investigate them.

1. Look closely at the price you've paid for food over the past three months. If there was an increase in the price you are paying for food, maybe the increase was an oversight on the part of your salesperson. If so, he owes you credit for the overpriced items.

2. Spend a few days watching your waste. Is this area completely under control? Do you have new employees who tend to waste more food than your seasoned employees?

3. How is your portion control? Are your employee's paying attention in this area? Are you?

4. Look at your inventory. Have you unknowingly let your inventory rise?

With these problems, a price increase is not the answer. More often than not, you can merely tighten your controls over one or more of these areas to avoid raising your prices.

If you find that all your controls are in place, and that the price increase you are paying for food is real and permanent, you must take action. When profits are down and every area of your food cost is under control, except the price you are paying for food, it's time for that price increase.

How Much to Increase Your Prices
If your food cost is normally 31.5%, but over the past three months your food cost has risen to 33.7%, then your food cost is out of line by 2.2%. If your net sales are $50,000, multiply this by 2.2% and you'll find that you need to recapture $1100 in food costs per month. In order to accomplish this, divide 100 by 31.5 (your food cost percentage) and you'll get 3.17. Now, multiply 3.17 by $1100 to get 3487. Your price increase must add $3487 to your net sales each month to lower your food cost by $1100.

Independents many times are afraid to have a price increase. They are afraid of losing good customers, but customers understand that you must increase your prices from time to time. Believe it or not, there is also a smart method to accomplish this, a way that your customers will appreciate.

Instead of having a sizable increase on several main menu items, one that everyone will notice, have a small across the board increase. In order to know how much to increase each item, you must know how much of each item you sell each month. How many orders of fries, how many medium drinks and so on? If you just don't know, track every item on your menu for a month, and after a month you will know.

Add all of these totals together. Let's say that you sold 30,000 food items during the month. If you need to increase your sales by $3487 through a price increase, then divide 3487 by 30,000 and you will get .1162. So, if you increase the price of every food item on your menu by about 11 and-a-half cents you would recapture $3487 per month, which would lower your food cost by $1100. Since you can't charge a half-cent, you may consider rounding down to 10 cents per item. While you will not recapture all of the money you need, you will recover more than 85% of it.

Chapter 6
Accounting

A Must

This little section, in my estimation, is one of the most important and the most overlooked areas of operating a successful independent restaurant. You cannot find success in this business without a CPA.

In fact, before opening your dream restaurant, or when you want to straighten out your current restaurant, there are two key tips I consider essential to achieving success.

1. You must have a CPA. I'm not talking about a friend who is a part-time bookkeeper; I'm talking about a Certified Public Accountant.

2. You must not take money out of your restaurant "under the table". Pay your taxes and operate an honest business, or there is little hope for you.

Many independents say, "I'll do my own accounting. I don't want anyone to know my business." What they don't understand is that by keeping others from knowing their business, they are also keeping themselves from knowing their business. The restaurant business is about control: your CPA's job is to help put you in control.

You can find a good CPA in the yellow pages of your telephone book. Most CPA's will charge a flat monthly fee of around $150 plus an additional charge for annual tax returns and w-2 forms. This may seem outrageous to you, but what's outrageous to me is the thought of you trying to operate a restaurant without a CPA. Here is what you can expect from your CPA.

1. Fill out all tax statements for you and compute all taxes.
    A. Payroll tax, FICA and FED
    B. Sales tax – State and local
    C. Quarterly taxes (payroll)
    D. All end-of-year reports and tax returns (produce W-2 forms)

2. Submit the Profit and Loss statement to you every month.

The monthly P&L statement is the one tool that can give you the control you need to find success in the restaurant business. When you decided to open your restaurant, you must have had a goal in mind. In order to reach a tool, you must first know where you are. A Profit and Loss statement will show you exactly where you are each and every month.

It's critical to your operation for your profit and loss statement to be accurate. The accuracy of your statement is in your hands. Each time you write a check, you must decide which account this money should be entered into. For instance, if you write a check for milk, you should code this check "Food" on your check stub. This tells your accountant to put the total of this check into food cost on your Profit and Loss statement.

How To Use a Profit & Loss Statement

If you've been operating a restaurant that has seen serious financial problems, then the day you get your first P&L statement will be a glorious day for you. Now, you will be able to pinpoint many of your problems. Can you believe it? A simple and inexpensive process like this can finally tell you what is wrong. Let's get to it.

Your P&L statement will arrive each month with a cover sheet. This sheet tells you that your accountant did not supply the information for this report, you did. It also explains that he or she cannot be held responsible for the content. He or she was only taking your word. The first page will cover your assets and the next page will cover your liabilities. Page three is your income statement. This is the page with which you will be most concerned.

The first item listed on the income statement will be your gross sales for last month. This should be of particular concern to you since your sales will be a major contributor to your success or failure. Your sales should always have an increase from the previous year's sales for any given month. You should always set sales goals – daily, weekly and monthly. The next item listed will be your sales tax owed and then your net sales. Net sales are your gross sales minus sales tax. Your P&L statement will then break down your expenses or the amount of money you spent in each account last month.

Food Costs

Your P&L statement will show you exactly the amount of money you spent on food for the month. It will also show you the percentage of sales which went into the cost of food.

For example: Your net sales for last month were $37,658. The total dollars you spent for food was $12,679, or 33.7% of your sales. This means every time you made a dollar in sales, you spent 33.7 cents of that dollar to buy food.

If you're in a full service restaurant, I'd say that your food cost is in great shape. If you're in a fast food restaurant, 33.7% is a little high. For an independent fast food restaurant, 31 or 32% would probably be more like it. So, if your food cost is 33.67% and you want it to be 31.5%, that's a difference of 2.17%. Multiply your net sales by 2.17% and you'll find that you spent $817.19 more than you should have spent on food. That's $817.19 that you can learn to put in your pocket. (Control) – isn't it fabulous? Refer to the PROFITS section of this book to learn how to control your food costs. Without a P&L statement you wouldn't even know that you had a food cost problem. By spending $150 this month for your CPA, you've found a way to capture $817.19 in only one of your accounts. Follow this same procedure for all the accounts on your P&L to find the total dollars you can capture with experience.

Account Percentage Guidelines

The National boys all have guidelines to follow which have been developed over the years. The poor independent has none. I'm going to give you an estimate of the percentages each of your accounts should be so you can use them as your guidelines. Remember, these guidelines will vary depending upon what type of restaurant you have.

Food cost	**32.00%**
Supply cost	**4.00%**
Labor cost	**22.00%**
Rent	**5.00%**
Repairs	**1.00%**
Accounting	**0.50%**
Advertising	**2.00%**
Insurance	**1.50%**
Linen	**0.40%**
Telephone	**0.25%**
Utilities	**3.50%**
Payroll taxes	**4.00%**
Interest	**1.50%**
Depreciation	**1.25%**
Taxes & License	**.75%**
Pest control	**0.05%**
Shortage	**0.00%**
Total Expenses	**79.70%**
Net Profit	**20.30%**

$40,000
20.30%
____
$8,120

If you could reach these goals each month, your net profit would be 20.3%. This means 20.3% of your net sales was profit. If your net sales for this month were $40,000, this would be multiplied by your net profit (20.3%)

How does $8,120 sound for a monthly income? With sales increases and tighter controls, this figure could move upward drastically. On the other hand, with lower sales and less control, the $8120 could disappear quickly.

Let me show you what could happen to your profit and loss statement when your sales change.

Net Sales $50,000

Food cost	**32.00%**
Supply cost	**4.00%**
Labor cost	**22.00%**
Rent	**2.00%**
Repairs	**0.80%**
Accounting	**0.40%**
Advertising	**2.00%**
Insurance	**1.20%**
Linen	**0.30%**
Telephone	**0.20%**
Utilities	**2.80%**
Payroll taxes	**4.00%**
Interest	**1.20%**
Depreciation	**1.00%**
Taxes & License	**0.60%**
Pest control	**0.05%**
Shortage	**0.00%**
Total Expenses	**76.50%**
Net Profit	**23.50%**

$50,000
x23.5%
$11,750

WOW! What a difference. By increasing your sales by $10,000 per month you have increased your income by $3,630. Not bad. Refer to the "Sales" chapter in this book to learn how to increase your sales.

As you will notice, the only accounts, which changed with this sales increase, were your fixed payments. Now, let me show you what can happen to your profits when there is very little control.

Net Sales $40,000

Food cost	**34.50%**
Supply cost	**5.50%**
Labor cost	**24.30%**
Rent	**5.00%**
Repairs	**1.50%**
Accounting	**0.50%**
Advertising	**3.50%**
Insurance	**1.50%**
Linen	**1.00%**
Telephone	**4.00%**
Utilities	**4.50%**
Payroll taxes	**5.00%**
Interest	**1.50%**
Depreciation	**1.25%**
Taxes & License	**0.75%**
Pest control	**0.05%**
Shortage	**0.00%**
Total Expenses	**99.35%**
Net Profit	**0.65%**

$40,000
x.65%
$260

Where did the profits go? The guy with the $260 profit had better learn control or he will be out of business soon. When I look at this expense page, I see a restaurant running itself, but a restaurant cannot make a profit alone. Someone must take control.

Let's go down this expense page and I'll briefly explain the problems.

Food Costs
The price paid for food could be too high. Menu prices too low. Too much waste. Portions out of control. Too much inventory.

Supplies
The price paid for paper products could be too high. Menu prices too low. Too much waste. Too much inventory

Labor Cost
Hourly wages too high. Poor scheduling. No adjustment to lower sales. Need better training program.

Repairs
Not changing air conditioning filters each month. Not cleaning coils on refrigeration equipment each month. Not cleaning and caring for equipment properly

Advertising
Sales in this restaurant would increase more quickly if the operator were to spend more time with the operation, and less

money on advertising. Advertising will not help a sloppy operation.

Linen

Not rationed to employees properly. Apparently, the linen is not locked up and everyone has free access to it.

Telephone

Yellow Page advertising should have been coded as advertising instead of a telephone expense. Too many long-distance phone calls. Needs to get to work and talk less.

Utilities

Not turning equipment on properly. Not cleaning coils on refrigeration equipment each month. Not changing a/c filters each month. Equipment working too hard. Not turning lights off when not needed. Not turning equipment on properly. Leaving walk-in door ajar.

Payroll taxes

These are up because payroll is up.

Shortage

No control. No one is counting registers after each shift.

Each one of these accounts is explained in depth in the PROFITS chapter of this book.

Are you beginning to see how a Profit & Loss statement can put you in control? It's so easy and well worth the accounting fee you will pay each month.

If you can identify where your money is going, you can begin to control it. Without a P&L statement, you are in the dark and will never see the success you had hoped to achieve.

Chapter 7
Other Pitfalls To Avoid

Lease Agreement

Before you negotiate a lease, term and price there are a few things you must consider. The first year a restaurant is open is the most critical year of all. The first 12 months you're open may determine how long you stay open.

So, it is very important to negotiate the lowest rent possible. Your landlord may already know how much he needs and wants as his rent amount. However, they also want you to be successful and will sometimes be willing to work with you. While negotiating the price, don't be so pushy that you give your landlord second thoughts about you to the point that he decides not to work with you.

You may find your landlord would be willing to let you operate at a lower rate the first year, if you allow him to raise the rent the second year. This may be very beneficial to you during the first critical year.

Try very hard to get a short-term lease with an option to extend. For example, you could negotiate a two-year lease with two, five-year options with the same terms. This means you will guarantee the rent for two years and if things don't work out you are free to leave after two years. If things do work out, you will have the option to stay for ten more years with all the same terms as the first two years.

By using these two methods, you have lowered your risk. Naturally, landlords love long-term leases, but many are very flexible. If you're dealing with a company-owned piece of property, or property that is owned by a group of investors, you may find negotiations won't go your way. If so, you must decide if the location is really worth what they are asking. Is it worth it to you?

Rent for a restaurant should be 5% of your net sales or less. Let's say your projected monthly net sales are to be $40,000 per month, and the landlord wants $2500 per month as rent. Simply divide 2,500 by 40,000 and you will find that your rent will be 6.25% of your sales. That is 1.25% higher than I recommend. That 1.25% of $40,000 represents $500 out of your pocket each and every month. That may not sound like a lot to you, however, you cannot give away very many five-hundred-dollar bills and expect to survive. Maybe you'll be unlucky and your sales will be lower than projected. If so, you will be in big trouble.

The decisions you make during these negotiations may make or break your future in the restaurant business. The one exception which would make the $2,500 rent, with $40,000 net sales look attractive would be if equipment were included with the building. Then it could be justified because your initial investment on equipment would be lower.

Be smart and be careful. Always have an attorney look over your lease agreement before signing unless you have knowledge of leases. Before leasing a building, you should try to get some guarantee on the roof, heat and air conditioning systems, and the plumbing and electrical. Also, please make sure the parking lot is in good shape. These are not things you need to deal with after you're open.

Many landlords will only lease a building "as is". This means no guarantees. Some will guarantee that all these things are in good working order. It would be a good idea for you to call a general contractor and have him check items out for you. It will cost you a little now, but it could cost much more later.

Capital
It's very common for an independent operator to consider all his cost for opening a new restaurant but to never think twice about having the capital on hand to operate the restaurant and to live on until the restaurant begins to make a profit. Most small businesses go under because they are under-capitalized. This means they did not have enough cash to hang on long enough to survive. Your new restaurant should open with $5,000 to $10,000 in the bank after all the expenses of your restaurant are paid. Never take your working capital out too soon! Leave this amount in your checkbook until your restaurant shows a strong profit: then cut your working capital down to $2,000 per month. I've found that after my restaurants are established and sound, $2,000 in working capital works fine. This enables you to begin

each month with $2,000, and that makes it very comfortable to manage your checkbook without juggling bills.

If you're already open and were under-capitalized when you opened, you may be experiencing some of the financial pains I've mentioned. If so, maybe you should take on an investor. How to do this is addressed in the "Financing" chapter. It may be practical for you to give up a small percentage of your business in order to save the entire business. Every business deserves a chance. With the proper amount of working capital your business will have its chance. I cannot stress how important working capital is to a restaurant, especially in the beginning.

Taxes

Taxes can be a very serious problem for the independent. Operate your business like a business. Some say, "I'll take out $100 or so every day and then I won't have to pay taxes on it. While they're busy trying to beat the government out of tax money, they're laying a blueprint for failure. A real business doesn't operate in that manner. You see, while they're taking money out of their operation, they're distorting the numbers on their P&L statement. When this happens, no one can help them, because the Profit & Loss statement will not be accurate.

The Profit & Loss statement will show you exactly how you're doing in each area of your restaurant, such as labor costs, food costs and so on, but if you IF you report accurate numbers to your accountant, but if you're taking cash out of your restaurant, these percentages will be higher than they normally would be and you will have no idea where you really are in terms of finances.

I've written this book to help independents operate a successful and profitable restaurant. If you want to save taxes by taking cash out of your restaurant and not reporting all of your sales, then you have wasted your money by buying this book. Pay your taxes and run a real business.

Building Appearance

When you rent a building, you must change the outside appearance. If you don't change the outside, how will people know you are open? Cars have passed this building for months or years and they are conditioned not to pay any attention to this location at all. You must make some cosmetic changes such as paint, plants, and flags on a rope, or anything, which will attract attention. The more change done, the better.

Signs

Don't open without a sign! Don't think that other independents haven't done this. It happens all the time, in fact, recently I saw and independent open a burger restaurant. There were no changes made to the building and no sign out front. One day the building was empty: the next day the restaurant was open. No one knew it was open except the owner and the employees. Now I ask you, what chance does this restaurant have? You must have a sign out front.

These are the most common mistakes made by the independent. These areas will totally paralyze your operation, giving you no chance for success. If you're about to open your restaurant, give yourself the chance you need and tackle these areas before you open.

If you're already open, there is still hope

1. You're still open. As long as you're still open, it's not too late to correct these past mistakes.

2. If you're just too broke to solve these problems, but you've finally decided to try to operate in a more businesslike manner, get the money. Go to a finance company for a loan. Cash in or borrow from your insurance policy. Ask your bank if you can skip a note payment. Ask your mortgage company if you can skip a house payment. Ask the company that financed your car if you can skip a payment. Use your credit card for cash. Raise the Money you need today!

I'm not saying you should get yourself deeper in debt without a plan. I'm just saying that if you've decided that you can turn your business around by making a few changes, but you're broke. There is money available if you try.

Chapter 8
Running Your Business

Daily Routine

Being organized and having the right work habits in the restaurant business will be critical to your success. A daily organizer is one of those forms that can and will help to organize you and your business. This organizer will consist of things that you can expect to happen each day of the week.

Example:

Monday
Bread – delivery
Milk – delivery
Tomato – delivery
Kraft Foods – order

Tuesday
Bread – delivery
Kraft Foods – delivery

Wednesday
Open

Thursday
Bread – delivery
Tomato – delivery
Kraft Foods – order

Friday
Bread – delivery
Kraft Foods – delivery
Milk – delivery

Saturday
Bread – delivery

With this organizer you'll know what to expect each day and you won't have any surprises. Another very important tool for you to use would be a monthly bill organizer.

Example:

Monthly Bills

	Item:	Check #:	Amount:
1st	Rent	1351	$1,250.00
2nd	Payroll	1352-1382	$4,481.00
4th	Utilities	1383	$1,277.33
7th	Bank Note	1384	$321.77
15th	Payroll	1385-1404	$4,631.15
18th	Insurance	1405	$261.00
20th	Sales Tax	1406	$3,175.00

Every monthly bill your restaurant has should be listed on this chart. List each item in order of the due date. This could be a very helpful tool for you. It could help you to plan your spending for each month. As you pay each bill, simply fill in the date paid; check number and the balance owed (if necessary). The balance of notes owed will be listed on your P&L. Clip these charts to a clipboard and hang near your desk for easy access.

Many times, when a person begins to work for him or herself, bad habits will creep into their lives. It's important to develop a professional daily routine, one, which will eliminate the destructive habits of operators who are bored or just don't know what needs to be done each day.

Example:

9:00am Have crew begin prep. Determine prep levels and monitor their progress.

9:30am Go to bank and pick up last night's deposit bag. Get enough change for today's operation.

10:00am Check on prep progress. Deal with salespeople or deliveries.

10:30am Have prep completed and begin clean up.

11:00am Prep completed and store clean. Begin to mentally prepare crew for lunch. Assure that everything is stocked up and ready for lunch business. Check crew's appearance and smiles.

11:30am Organize and supervise lunch.

1:00pm Monitor clean up and re-stocking.

2:00pm Lunch for you and your crew.

2:30pm Organize afternoon prep and clean up. Monitor customer service and quality of food.

5:00pm Organize shift change. Count cash drawers for shortage. Run sales report. Figure labor cost.

5:30pm Mentally prepare crew for dinner business. Remind crew of customer service and quality of food. Monitor, organize and supervise dinner.

8:30pm Monitor closing clean up.

9:00pm Monitor closing clean up. Begin nightly reports, daily reports and labor sheets.

Closing
Complete daily report and labor sheets. Count cash of shortage. Make night deposit. Check your crew out. Make sure everything is stored properly. Complete daily inventory. Check all doors to make sure they are locked. Drive to bank and make night deposit.

For you to make the kind of profits you want, you must operate your restaurant as a business. A professionally operated restaurant, which has net sales of $40,000 per month, could earn you more than $10,000 per month in profits. You won't be able to have those types of results in a month or two. The exciting part of this is the progress you'll see each month. As you become more and more confident and educated on these matters, your sales and profits will grow.

Your Desk

There are two types of operators of restaurants. There's the "Hands on" operator, who helps his crew in every area of the restaurant. Then there's the "Desk" operator, who spends most of his time at his desk planning, thinking and figuring. I'm not saying the "Desk" operator is bad, but as I said in an earlier chapter, who knows what your crew, is doing while you're lost in paper work at your desk?

I hope, by now, that you've decided to operate a businesslike operation and that you control each area of your business. Your crew will always demand the most attention. While deskwork is important to your success, pick your desk time wisely.

There are several things you will need at your desk in order to operate your restaurant. The first year or so, you will need a current picture of your family on your desk since you may not see them as often as before.

Seriously, you will need a payroll book. This can be purchased at any office supply store. As you hire employees, write their names in the payroll book. Under their names, write their addresses and social security numbers. When you write their first payroll checks, also list their addresses and social security numbers on the check stub for your accountant. Your accountant must have this information for tax purposes. Remember that you only need to list this information on each employee's first check stub.

Next, you will need some type of a file for your employee's applications. This file will need to have three sections – one for current employees, one for ex-employees and one for applicants who were not hired. As employees leave your employment, move their applications from current to ex-employee. Stay organized!

Next, you'll need a calculator. You will also need a calendar, daily reports (available from your accountant), envelops, deposit slips, stamps, your monthly bill organizers and daily organizer sheets. You will also need a stapler, paper clips, pens, pencils, a cash box, file folders, night deposit bags and keys (from your bank), employee work schedules, inventory folders (from your supplier) and of course, your checkbook.

Any filing system you decide on will be great. You will however, need three very important folders. One for unpaid bills, one for bills paid and one for daily reports.

At the end of each month, send your daily reports and check stubs for the month to your accountant. Your accountant will prepare your tax forms and your P&L. Then, she'll send them back to you. She will also send your daily reports and check stubs back to you.

At the end of the month, you will need to empty your "bills paid" folder and store them as records. When your daily reports and check stubs are returned, they should also be stored with your bills paid for that particular month as "records".

The best policy you could ever establish, as an independent, is to pay for everything as it comes in. With enough working capital, this can be easily accomplished. By paying in this manner, you will never owe anyone and will avoid many of the financial problems that independents face every day. It takes discipline,but you can do it.

I was helping a group of franchise operators a few years ago to deal with some of their operational problems. Some of the best advice I gave them was for them to pay their bills and keep their "unpaid bills" folders empty.

Each of them had a tremendous number of unpaid bills. They took my advice, paid their bills and began a policy of staying current with their bills. A few months later, I talked with them and they told me that their "new" system of paying bills worked like magic. It streamlined their system and made their businesses very easy to understand. When a person can understand something, he or she can begin to control it.

Folks, I'm telling you, you will have a very difficult time in this business if you do not stay current on ALL of your bills. If you just cannot get current or stay current, you may consider an investor or a bank loan. You will not begin to see the progress you hoped for until this problem is solved.

Chapter 9
Profits

Controlling Expenses

Profits are the reason we're in business and you have the opportunity every month to increase your income. If you want a raise, all you have to do is decide and make it happen. This, to me, is the most exciting chapter of this book. You will learn some simple and exciting ways to increase your profits and give yourself that raise you need and deserve. Combine this chapter with the accounting chapter and you'll have a very explosive combination. If you were to exchange the word "profits" with the word "control", you'd get a better picture of profits. By placing the proper controls in **every** area of your restaurant, your profits will be high.

There are nine basic areas on your P&L statement over which you have some control. You should review this chapter several times each month until every word becomes a part of your everyday thinking. This is the chapter that will make you the money you have dreamed of. They are:

Food costs
Supply costs
Labor costs
Repairs

Advertising
Linen
Telephone
Utilities
Shortage

Food Costs

Let's slow your operation down for a minute and really take a hard look at your food cost.

There are four ways to control your food cost.

1. The price you pay will always be a main consideration for you. Remember that an independent needs two suppliers in order to keep prices competitive. Always think quality and never change a product or sacrifice quality for price. Get the lowest price possible and constantly monitor this price as your salesperson could raise the price without your knowledge.

You never want to sell an inferior product, but you do want to sell every piece of what you buy, or else you want to receive credit for it. Let's say that in a box of tomatoes you find six tomatoes, which are simply not usable. Save these tomatoes for your salesperson and he will give you credit for them. Any product, which you buy that is, damaged, spoiled or just not usable, should be credited back to you. Sometimes tomatoes cost 35 cents each, or more, so it becomes very important to stay on top of this critical area.

Always check your order in when it arrives. Make sure everything you paid for is there. Truck drivers sometimes miss items and leave them on their truck. If you sign this invoice or pay the bill, you are saying that the order was all there. It is critical for you to pay attention to each delivery. Before you sign or pay the invoice, run down each item to make sure you are being charged the price quoted by your salesperson. If you are paying C.O.D., you must handle this with the driver. The driver will call the office and try to get it straightened out. Always check the price you're paying for each item before paying an invoice.

Most operators look at the entire picture instead of a small part of it. For example, a restaurant may buy and shred seven or eight cases of lettuce per week. Since that's a lot of lettuce, a small handful may seem unimportant. But if you take care of each handful of every item you purchase, you will not have a food cost problem. Remember that your goal is to sell very piece of each item you buy, or to receive credit for it.
If you're going to run a special, ask your supplier to help you with free product for the promotion. For an ice cream special your dairy company might let you have a case or two of free ice cream for the promotion. Remember that you're going to promote their product ant that will also help them.

The price you pay for food is the largest percentage of your costs each month. The higher your sales, the more power you will have to lower the price you pay. If you only spend $300 or $400 each week with your supplier, you'll have very little power, but if you spend $1000 or more each week, you can demand a lower price. If you spend this much simply go to your supplier and ask for a price decrease by telling the supplier that you feel you are paying too much for food. Ask and you shall receive.

2. Waste is an area you will always need to address. Your employees will tend to cook a few extra fries just to make sure they have enough for the order. The extra fries they cook but don't use is called waste. You bought it, you paid for it and now you will throw it away. When you went through your menu pricing procedure, you didn't allow for waste. You must stop waste of all kinds.

Learn to save money during prep. For instance, if you make your own onion rings and you also chop onions for burgers, never chop a whole onion for the burger. Instead, slice the onion for your onion rings and use the center of the onion to chop. The center cannot be used for onion rings, but they are fine to chop for burgers. So, you waste none of the onion, because there is nothing to throw away.

Another example is to save the ends of tomatoes that would normally end up in the garbage can and use them in your chili. Or chop them and put them in your vegetable soup. There is value in the ends of your tomatoes. Find a use for them. Learn to stretch your food to higher profits.

Make sure your prep levels are accurate. If you prepare too much lettuce today it could brown overnight and you'd have to throw it away? If you slice too many tomatoes today, they will not be fresh tomorrow. So, you should prepare produce twice a day. Prepare enough in the morning to last through mid afternoon, and enough in the afternoon to last until closing. This will allow you to sell the freshest produce possible.

You can also cut waste by saving all damaged food. If you have a slice of toast, or a bun, which cannot be used, save it for your supplier. Maybe it came out of the package in bad condition. Maybe your crew or the bakery overcooked it. Regardless of the reason for the damage, save it and receive credit for it. You can normally get credit for a tray of bread every two or three days by saving all you bad or damaged bread.

Employees should never be allowed to eat their mistakes without paying for them. If they are allowed to do so they may make mistakes just to eat free. Have an employee eating policy, such as soft drinks free and ice cream or food ½ price while on duty.

Have you ever noticed your kitchen floor after a busy period? It can be covered with food – food that you paid for. You may think this is the nature of the business, but I disagree. It's a training problem. You can train your crew to drop less food on the floor where it will only be swept up and thrown away. If it's important to you, then it will be important to your employees.

Are you getting the message? Every speck of food you buy only makes money if it's sold. Stop food from ending up in your trash can. All you have to do is to decide to control every morsel of every item you buy and then make it happen.

3. Portion control is a very important factor. If you've determined that four ounces of fries constitutes an order, use containers, which will only hold four ounces of fries. Larger than average portions should never be tolerated. Remind your employees that raises are generated from stopping waste and portion control is a large part of controlling waste.

I've seen customers ask for extra napkins and an employee will give them a handful. Anytime a customer asks for anything extra and an employee acts as if there is an abundance of it, that item becomes waste. These behaviors will cost you money – *your* money. Train your employees to give only a reasonable amount of whatever.

4. Inventory is the most important and least-used method of protecting your food investment. Remember that 29 to 38 cents of every dollar earned by your restaurant will be spent to purchase your food.

Inventory is used to educate you on your daily and weekly usage of each food item you purchase and will benefit you greatly when ordering your food. If one box of meat costs you $28.00, you can see how you could quickly have a great deal of money tied up in unnecessary inventory. Lower inventory means increased profits.

Inventory helps you to pinpoint exactly what you need to order, which keeps you from under ordering or over ordering. Inventory also helps you to keep theft under control. If you have twenty boxes of meat in your freezer, a questionable employee may find it easy to take one box home with him. If you only have two boxes of meat on hand, this employee may think twice about it.

If your sales are strong enough, you may consider ordering daily. This keeps your inventory very low and your products very fresh.

You can obtain inventory folders from your supplier. Here's how they work.

Daily
Inventory

Date:	8/9	8/10	8/11	8/12	8/13	8/14	8/15
Fries							
Corn							
Cheese							
Cups							
Lettuce							

List each item on the left side. I would list these items on this folder in the order you have them stored. This method will simplify your inventory procedures. An example would be to list everything in your walk-in cooler from the left side, top and bottom shelves in order, all the way around your cooler to the right side. This method will make inventory simple. You wouldn't want to inventory something in the cooler and then go to your freezer for the next item listed and then back to the cooler.

The top triangle is for what you have used. To find this out, simply subtract today's "on hand" from yesterdays "on hand". One thing to remember, this inventory should always take place after closing for the day.

When you receive a delivery, this must be added to yesterdays "on hand". After a week has passed, you'll know your daily usage of each item.

If anything is missing, you'll know because your usage of that particular item will go up. If sales increase, each item will also increase.

Most independents will not inventory because it is time consuming. However, daily inventory will absolutely put you in control of your food costs.

Supply Costs

Daily inventory should also take place with your supply items (paper goods). Inventory will put you in touch with your daily usage of each item and in control of your ordering. If a case of cups costs $18.00, then you can have a great deal of money tied up in unnecessary inventory by over-ordering.

A few tips concerning your paper supplies. Don't clean up a mess with a napkin because they cost money. Use a cloth towel instead. If a drink for an order is duplicated, don't throw the cup away. Rinse it out and use it for the next order. Begin to understand, no matter how small the item, you paid for it. If it is wasted, you get to throw it away and buy another.

Take care of the pennies and the dollars will take care of themselves.

Labor Costs

This expense will be the second-largest expense in your restaurant each month, second only to food cost. As an independent, you can expect your labor costs to be 22% or more of your net sales.

Waste is also prevalent in this area. What will be wasted is time. Time you are paying for. Some things to remember are, a busy employee is a happy employee. When you have more help than work, gossip sets in. When this happens, the results will always be negative. Keep your employees busy, you'll both be glad you did.

Turnover in our business is very common and also very expensive. Turnover is where you constantly hire and train new employees over and over again. You must learn how to cut down your turnover. When you first hire an employee, his or her contribution to your operation is tiny. This means that for several days, or for a couple of weeks, these new employees are an extra expense to you.

During new employees training period the new employee will also waste more food and paper supplies than a trained crewmember will. A new cashier may also unintentionally give away your money. Your customers and trained employees do not enjoy a new crewmember any more than you do. If you constantly have a new and untrained crewmember handling your customers, the customer may become irritated and begin to eat someplace else. Your customers are looking for a professional crew and are not interested in the confusion that a new crewmember can cause.

I'd advise that you do all the training yourself. By doing this you can monitor everything the new employee does. It will enable you to somewhat shield your customers and trained crew from the confusion a new crewmember can create. By training your employees yourself you will open the lines of communication between you and them. It will also enable you to teach this new employee exactly the way you want things done.

All employees learn at a different pace, but you cannot afford to keep an employee very long who is unable to make a positive contribution to the operation. An employee with a great attitude and the desire to learn is whom you want to find. These people are worth taking the time to really train. The ones who have selfish attitudes are the ones who will give you problems.

Remember that you are the one who advertised for someone to help you! You did not advertise for someone you could help. As long as the new employee has a good attitude, learns quickly and honestly wants to help you accomplish your objectives, you will have a great working relationship.

Your employees need a pat on the back more than they need a raise. Employees always need to feel appreciated. This does not mean that you should hand out unwarranted praises. Only praise an employee for a good job when they actually do a good job. When they do, you should be the first to recognize it. You must understand that your employees want to do a good job. They want to please you and to make you proud of them. They want you to win. They love to work for a winner and the busier you stay with sales building and profit building, the more of a winner you will appear to be.

If your employees have faith in you, they will stay up day and night trying to help you. Remember this, for a very small amount of money; each crew member is working to help you become successful. You cannot operate without them, but they can operate without you. They can always find another job to replace the small amount of money you're paying them.

You must learn how to motivate your employees and develop loyalty for them. A price cannot be placed on loyalty. You loyal crewmembers will be the backbone of your operation and should always be recognized as such. The more loyal employees you have, the less turnover you will have. This means higher profits and increased sales.

Keep your and your crew's focus on the restaurant. If the restaurant wins, everyone wins. If not, everyone loses. Everyone has a hand in the restaurant's success and each individual must be aware of this. Instill a sense of pride among your crewmembers. This sense of pride begins with you. You crew will always be a reflection of you. If you have winning qualities and a winning attitude so will your crew.

When I began managing, I was the top operator in a growing national fast-food chain. I was so good that I was a very difficult manager to work for. I demanded everything to be done exactly like I wanted. I also demanded it be done right now! I was a terror. My attitude was "If you can't do it or won't do it, I'll get someone who will. "To all those employees who worked for me then, I apologize now.

You see I was young and probably a little scared. I wanted to win so badly that I thought the only way to do that was to force employees to do that I wanted at any cost to them. As the years passed, I realized that employees respond to your wishes better if they respect you. They respond to your needs even better if you respect them and recognize their accomplishments.

You and your crew are in this together. You're a team working together to accomplish certain goals. You are the captain or quarterback of this team. It's your job to always put the best team on the field; however, each team member must play and contribute. As long as everyone does his or her job well your team will win.

You must understand that occasionally someone will drop the ball and your team will suffer a setback. This is when you, your team and the person who dropped the ball will have to regroup and get back out on the field. In life, as in sports, dropping the ball too many times cannot be tolerated. Each team member has a responsibility to the entire team.

Your team must have faith in your ability to lead. If they do, they will give their heart and soul to the team. If they don't, they will become disinterested and preoccupied with other things. This will cause them to drop the ball more often. When this happens, you may need to trade this player to another team. Maybe he really needed to be traded. Maybe it was actually you who caused the trade to be necessary.

When an employee becomes disinterested in his or her job, it could be a personal distraction, which has nothing to do with you or the job. You should bring this to his or her attention and try to solve the problem before it begins to affect your business. They should be made to understand that your business is no place for personal problems. Mistakes can destroy a business. You must offer your customers things they cannot receive anyplace else. One of those things could be no mistakes with their order. Mistakes occur when crewmembers do not focus or concentrate on what they are doing. This is a form of dropping the ball. This type of repeated behavior cannot be tolerated. Make your goal – NO MISTAKES.

Picture this. Your customer has placed a large to-go order. With complete trust in you, the customer does not check the order before driving to the other side of town. When they arrive and check the order, they realize that some of the order is missing. Can you imagine the frustration? Your customer is hungry and tired. They don't want to drive all the way across town again, especially since it was your mistake. The customer calls to complain. What do you do?

Let's stop and think this over for a minute!

You could do what every other restaurant does – give credit on his or her next visit to your restaurant. Or……you could do the RIGHT thing. Remake the entire meal and take it to your customer. What other restaurant would do that? None right?

Back to the problem. Because someone was not paying attention, your customer was irritated. The order had to be reproduced at your expense and you had to make a delivery across town. Wouldn't it be faster and better for everyone to slow down and do things the right way? Remind your crew before each busy period to concentrate and keep mistakes low.

As stated previously, your crew will be the most difficult area you will have to handle throughout your restaurant career. Learning how to deal with people and solve problems can keep stress in check and put fun into your life. Read books and listen to motivational tapes for help in this area.

I once wrote a complicated manual on labor cost. There's much to be said. There are forms and formulas which can be used to give the operator complete control of labor costs. I won't, however, get into those things in this book, as I don't think the independent operator has as much interest in those things as national operators do.

You, as an independent, do need to learn how to compute your labor cost. By doing this, you can begin to discover which part of the day your labor is costing you the most. Then you will be able to control that part of the day.

If you wanted to compute your labor percentage for lunch, you must first determine exactly how much you spent for employees. Multiply each employee's hours worked during lunch by his or her hourly rate of pay.

Add each employee's total pay for lunch and divide this by your net sales for lunch. Remember that net sales are your gross sales minus sales tax. This will give you the labor percentage for lunch.

In most cases, the labor percentage for lunch will be the lowest period of the day. Afternoon is normally very high and nights are usually moderate. Your goal for the day is 22%. However, you'll find that your labor percentages are normally lower on Friday and Saturday. This means that EVERY day does not need to be 22%. For instance, 24% labor cost on Monday and Tuesday may be all right, if your labor costs on Friday and Saturday are 20%.

You must begin to think in terms of percentages instead of dollars. Dollars will tell you how much you spent, but percentages will tell you if you spent too much or too little.

Don't think for one minute that if a crewmember is scheduled to work from 9 to 5, that you can't alter that. Maybe you can send them home at 4:45 or 4:30 if you're not busy.

Remember that money is only made when crewmembers are serving customers. If you have no customers during a period of time, labor costs will be high. The periods of time during a day when you have no customers are the areas you must control in order to control your labor costs.

Repairs
You can actually control, to some extent, the amount of money you spend on repairs. Here's how.

Change your air conditioning filters every thirty days. Every piece of refrigeration equipment you have has coils. Learn how to clean these coils. Do this every thirty days and these units will not break down nearly as often because they will not work nearly as hard.

Learn how to clean and maintain all your equipment. Employees tend to be rough on equipment, never giving any thought to the cost of it. Your employees must be taught to handle equipment gently, so it will last a very long time.

Advertising

There are thousands of ways to advertise. Since it is impossible for you to afford to advertise a thousand ways, you must find the most effective (meaning one which gives results) and the most economical. Your budget for advertising should be 2% or your net sales. Stay within your budget and learn how to say NO.

Linen

Unfortunately, towels and aprons must be rationed to your employees. One towel per employee per shift should be sufficient. Should an employee dirty these towels, they must learn to wash it out.

Telephone

I don't understand how anyone can make a long distance call on someone else's phone and think its O.K. You'll also need to monitor this area and have these culprits pay.

Advertising in the yellow pages has never made much money for me. It is, however, a large expense. I have a friend who advertised his business in the yellow pages. It cost him $265 per month each year. He felt as though he had made a terrible mistake and was so glad to see the year-end, so he could get out of the yellow pages and pay himself the $265 per month.

Utilities

Utility companies charge you based on your usage, but also there is a demand charge. For instance, if you turn all your equipment on at the same time, you create a huge demand. Try turning one piece of equipment on and then another two minutes later, and so on until everything is turned on. You'll see a nice savings. Also, by changing your air conditioning filters and cleaning the coils on your refrigeration equipment every thirty days, your equipment won't have to work as hard. If you do, your equipment will use less electricity.

Shortage

I have seen restaurants loose $2,000, even $3,000 per year to shortage. This can be controlled simply by making it a priority. Count your money after lunch and at shift change. Simply by making it seem important to you and to let others know you are watching, will cut this problem at least in half. I understand counting money three times a day is a hassle, but if it will save you $2,000 per year, it is worth it.

Are you beginning to get the picture? All you have to do is decide. If you decide you want a low phone bill or lower food costs or whatever, you can have it. But it has to be a goal of yours to make it happen. If you decide you want lower electric bills, you can have it. Just decide, set a goal and make it happen. Learn the power of control!

Chapter 10
Sales

Understanding Sales

In order to build sales, you must change your customers' eating habits. Customers may be in the habit of eating at several different places and leaving you off their list. Every customer has a favorite restaurant. What can you do to help your restaurant to become the favorite of more people?

1. You must have great food.

2. Your service and the level of enthusiasm of you and your crew must be exceptional.

3. Spruce up the outside of your restaurant.

    Cut the grass
    Sweep your parking lot
    Paint your building another color
    All outside signs working properly
    Clean windows
    Trim all bushes

4. Spruce up the inside of your restaurant.

   Paint the interior
   Have great looking carpet
   Give your restaurant a comfortable and relaxed atmosphere with plants
   Pay attention to the appearance of your crew
   Clean windows
   Attitudes of your crew should be positive with lots of enthusiasm and smiles
   Select great music for your dining room

Motivation and Enthusiasm

Answer these questions as honestly as you possibly can.

1. When someone asks you how you're doing, do you answer, "Great, fabulous or fantastic?" Or do you answer, "I'm fine, pretty good or I'm O.K."?

2. Does your crew get excited and happy when they see a customer pulling onto your parking lot, or do they get upset?

3. Look at your crew. What do you see?

   a. a lot of smiles
   b. a few smiles
   c. no smiles

4. Do you set sales goals from time to time?

5. Does your restaurant have regular hours, or do you sometimes open late or close early?

6. When you wake up in the morning are you anxious to get to your restaurant, or do you oversleep?

7. Do you ever find yourself wishing business would slow down from time to time so that you can do something else?

8. Does your crew call in sick, or are they late to work more often than they were last year?

9. During slow periods of the day are you thinking business thoughts or personal thoughts?

10. Are you ready to throw your hands up and run away to the Bahamas?

You know the CORRECT answer to all of these questions. If the truth forced you to answer any of these questions the wrong way, then we may have found your sales problem. You need a little motivation.

There are many motivational tapes out there. My suggestion is to buy some today. I have used Zig Ziglar during most of my career. I have also used many others, including Tony Robins. All of these guys have a powerful message waiting for you. I can tell you from experience, enthusiasm DOES make a tremendous difference.

In another chapter of this book, I touched on how important enthusiasm is in the business world. It is the best sales builder I have ever seen. Remember, anyone can sell food. But it's hard to find someone who loves to sell food. You know the ones I mean. They have waited on you before. Remember how they made you feel and how disappointed you were the next time you went to the same restaurant and they weren't there?

What would happen if you had a whole crew like that? You can…but it starts with you. YOU have to decide.

This should be a happy time in your life, not a miserable time. You own a restaurant and it's still open, so there's hope for you. Order your motivational tapes today. With a little enthusiasm and the knowledge from this book, you could change your entire situation from a negative one to a very positive one.

A great way to increase enthusiasm and increase sales is to learn the ART of suggestive selling. It's fun, a turn on for your customers and will add sales to your business. I used an example of a drive-thru crew member in a previous chapter. Now, let's use the same drive-thru crew member to sell.

Crew Member

Hi, welcome to Mel's may I take your order please?

Customer

Yes, I'd like an old-fashioned burger and that will be all.

Crew Member

All right ma'am
Would you like a slice of melted cheese on your burger?

Customer

Yes, that sounds good.

Crew Member

Fantastic, how about an order of fries or onion rings to go along with your burger? If you like onion rings, ma'am, we've got the best in town.

Customer

You sold me, what else do I want?

Crew Member

How about a thick and creamy chocolate milk shake?

Customer

Wow! You're a great salesman….I'll take it.

Crew Member

All right ma'am, I have an old-fashioned burger with cheese, an order of onion rings and a thick and creamy chocolate shake.

Customer

That's correct.

Crew Member

Fantastic ma'am, your total will be $4.79. Thanks, and you havea great night.

All your customer wanted in the beginning was a hamburger. Now, she's going home with an entire meal. It's fun. You cannot say these things to a customer with a dead-beat voice, you've really got to get into it. Loosen up and have some fun, but don't get too carried away. You must know your customers. With some customers, you'll need to back off a little but, generally, having fun attracts new customers.

This is only an illustration of what is possible. Play with this. Give it a try for an hour. What do you have to lose? Name another restaurant in your town that can, will or does deliver this type of enthusiasm. You can't, can you?

Overcoming "Low Volume Mentality"
The next problem with your sales may be what I call "Low volume mentality".

If you and your crew go to your restaurant each day, thinking, "It's going to be slow today. It was slow yesterday and it's going to be slow today also." Guess what? It's gonna be slow today! If you never expect it to be busier today than it was yesterday, then it probably won't be. Even if your restaurant tried to be busier, how could you and your crew handle it given the frame of mind you're in? Expectations are one of the most powerful tools I have ever seen. I don't mean for you to wish your sales up; I mean for you to expect them to increase and then do something about it. Don't just sit there and wait for them to go up, that won't happen. Expect it and then plan for it.

If your sales were to double tomorrow, would your current procedures be adequate? Here's an example. If you are in a low volume restaurant and you just realized that your coke tank was empty, the thoughts may be, "There's no rush. I will change the empty coke tank in a minute. In a high-volume restaurant, every time you get a chance, you check your syrup tanks. Change that attitude of, "Oh well, there's no rush" in your restaurant today!

Thinking like this will keep your restaurant at the low volume level. You must always be prepared to handle customers without running out of anything. Always be ready. ALWAYS!

When a customer orders, don't act like you've got all day. What if another customer was to order while your crew was dragging around with the first order? What would happen while you were napping? You see, every time you get an order, no matter what time of day, you should take care of it as if you were expecting three or four more right behind it. This is a very healthy attitude, which will change the entire atmosphere of your restaurant. If you are in a low-volume restaurant, you know exactly what I am saying.

Have you ever noticed; when your restaurant is busy, your employees have a sense of urgency about them. When you have one customer, your employees S..L..O..W down. It's almost as if they're saying that one customer is not as important as several. Did you know that if you take care of one customer with the same energy that you take care of several that soon you will always have several.

Be ready and expect more. Eventually, you will have more. If you were to do all the things discussed in this section, I can almost guarantee that in three months' time that you would see a major difference in sales.

Don't ever look at your situation as being dark and gloomy. Become a problem solver and begin to attack some of these very serious problems that you have. After you have changed those low-volume attitudes, decided to take control of the situation and gotten your crew mentally ready for more sales, your restaurant may need a nudge.

As you begin to accomplish these things, you'll feel differently. You'll feel great about your future. You'll feel as though something good is about to happen, and it will. Once you have completed all the above, you are ready to put a game plan into action.

Remember, you are trying to change people's eating habits. Their first experience at your restaurant is a very critical one toward changing their habits. When they leave your restaurant, your customer must feel happy, loved, pampered and important. Your job is to make them feel glad they ate at your restaurant.

Your customer may have had bad experiences all day long and it's your job to turn the day around for him or her. It's not just the meal, it's the entire experience. It's the enthusiasm and happiness of your crew; it's the music and the atmosphere. It's the entire experience.

Chapter 11
Sales Promotion Techniques

Simple and free

I'm not big on specials alone. I have never found that to be the answer. The only way they are effective is if I'm trying to accomplish a specific goal, such as introducing a new item. A good monthly special is a good idea. Have one special for the entire month and then change your special each month.

Having two or three specials going on at one time is confusing to your customers. You don't want to get yourself into a situation where you are expected to have a special or your customers will not stop by.

Specials will bring new customers to you, but when they arrive, it's up to you to dazzle them with your perfectly prepared food and enthusiastic service. If you do, there's a very good chance you'll see that customer again. Remember, if you keep on doing what you've been doing, you'll keep on getting what you've been getting. Decide to change today. Once you have this part down, the rest will come easily.

Develop three separate specials. Each of these will be "Buy one meal, get one free."

Example:

Full-Service Restaurant
#1 Buy one rib eye steak dinner get one free
#2 Buy one broiled chicken dinner get one free
#3 Buy one catfish dinner get one free

Fast Food Restaurant
#1 Buy one Burger meal get one free
#2 Buy one Ham sandwich meal get one free
#3 Buy on Fish sandwich meal get one free

Seem outrageous? We're trying to change habits here and it's no time to throw together a weak special which may or may not work. This is an investment in all of your tomorrows.

Flyers
Have 1,000 attractive and well-designed flyers printed for each special. Anytime you have flyers printed for a special, always have an expiration date printed on them. You don't want specials running indefinitely. If you have a three-week promotion, have special #1 expire on the 7th, #2 expire on the 14th and #3 expire on the 21st.

Try to target the flyers to new customers, customers who go elsewhere. Pass out flyers for special #1 and get ready. Great food and great service are critical now. Dazzle these new customers with your crew's newfound enthusiasm. When they arrive with their flyers, give them each a flyer for special #2.

When they come back, the second week, with flyer #2, give them flyer #3. If you're doing your job, these customers' entire experience at your restaurant should be good enough to change their habits after three visits.

Always keep in mind what you're trying to accomplish. This is not a promotion to see how much you can increase your sales. It's a promotion to change the eating habits of 1,000 people. Target these 1,000 people carefully and keep your focus on them at all times. If you can accomplish this you will have a very successful promotion which will reward you every day from here on out. If two or three weeks after your promotion you can maintain a ten to fifteen percent increase in your sales before the promotion, you did a very good job.

If your restaurant hasn't seen a customer in weeks, and your crew consists of you and your spouse, you may want to start with only 100 flyers. But, never have a promotion if you are understaffed. You'll do more harm than good, so hire and train new employees before distributing flyers.

This is one of many sales-building methods. There are many others, but each one must have one added ingredient in order to be effective. All must have enthusiasm to back up the method.

Another tactic is to have flyers of your menus printed. Have your crew place these in every business in town. The employees of almost every one of those businesses eat out for lunch. Factories, hospitals, automobile dealerships, utility companies, telephone companies and banks are all great targets. Basically, any place where you find people, you'll find opportunity. Don't sit in that building of yours another day waiting for sales to increase. It will never happen. You are going to have to go out there and get them.

I suppose that by now you realize that I believe in knocking on doors, shaking hands and kissing babies as my main technique for building sales. I believe that hard work in this area will give you the results you want and need. Most of my advertising dollars through the years have been spent on flyers and paper menus. With this we have always experienced great results, regardless of the type of restaurant.

Coupon Books

Coupon books are a great way for you to receive local exposure for your restaurant. Coupon books are put together by various groups. In a coupon book you can have four to six coupons. The cost to you is nothing, you must, however, give some food away with every coupon, such as, "buy one, get one free." Groups may sell a thousand coupon books for around $29.95 each. This means a lot of cheap exposure for your restaurant. If a person pays $29.95 for a coupon book, you can bet they will use every last coupon.

As always, when someone brings you a coupon, it's not negative, it's positive. Here's why and how to make the most of coupons.

#1. This customer is at your restaurant instead of at another. And that is where you wanted them to be when you put the coupon in the book.

#2. You now have a chance to show off your enthusiasm and excitement.

#3. With these coupons you are able to showcase any menu item. But always showcase your best seller. Don't coupon a weak seller because your coupon customer won't be happy.

#4. Don't hassle a customer with fine print. If your special is for a catfish dinner and your new customer wants steak instead, gladly let him have the steak. Be flexible. Remember what you're trying to accomplish. I've seen far too many places be too strict in this area for me. My attitude has always been, "I'm just glad you're here! Enjoy your steak."

Look Busy Become Busy
Have you ever noticed how people don't like to eat at an empty restaurant? If I'm driving by your restaurant and you have no cars in your parking lot, I won't stop. So, you should park your car on your parking lot and have your employees do the same. Now, with several cars on your parking lot, I will stop and eat.

Customers seem to run in crowds. If you get one customer, usually another is not far behind. By putting your car on the parking lot, it may lure a customer to you. While he is eating, another customer is likely to come along. Pretty soon, you may have a crowd.

Here's a good sales building idea. When it's slow and there are no customers, have a few of your employees clean the outside windows. Outside activities usually attract customers. Get out your water hose and water your plants. People are always attracted to water in the summer. Get your sprinklers going. Water, motion and summer, what a great combination.

You probably think that these suggestions are all so simple and wonder why you didn't think of them. It's because you were focused on the problem instead of the solution. By now you should be feeling excited and you should be realizing that there is hope for you. Now that you have been encouraged to be creative, what else can you do that is free and fun to increase your sales? Go ahead. I dare you to think of something on your own.

Free Advertising
Sometimes your restaurant will need a push. If you sit inside and wonder why your business is so slow, you'll never win. EVER! Take action now to make things happen in your life. Believe me, the list of free advertising can go as far as your creative juices will allow.

Here's a great idea. There is a way to advertise on the radio for free. No money required. Many radio stations have a lunch giveaway program. All you have to do is offer a free lunch for two to Mel's place to the fifth caller. These giveaways usually run on your radio station for one hour a day and they may giveaway six or eight meals a day. The exciting thing is all the free plugs your restaurant will receive during the hour. Take this one step further, and just before the giveaway begins send the D. J. your best menu item. Let the D. J. sample your food just before he or she goes on the air. Then count how many good things are said about the delicious food at your restaurant. I've used this method many times and I always get great results. I've also used barter for air time. Sometimes the radio station will trade air time for food. Only trade dollar for dollar. Ask and you shall receive.

Put a stack of your menus on the counter of every business in town. Almost every business will let you do this. Have you ever passed through a town on a trip and asked the service attendant to recommend a good place to eat? If your menus are there, they will probably recommend you. Learn how to persuade others to advertise for you.

When I first started in this business, I had a restaurant on the edge of downtown. Every morning, on my way to the bank, I would stop at three businesses to say hello. I wasn't there to buy, I was there to sell, but don't get me wrong, I didn't stop to ask them to have lunch at my restaurant, I stopped for a few seconds just to say "hi" and to get a smile from everyone. But I do admit that on my way out I would say, "See you later for lunch.

The most amazing thing would happen. Two out of three did in fact have lunch at my restaurant. It worked every time. Why do you think that happened? I think it worked because I was on their minds just before lunch. I always tried to get a laugh from everyone. Back in those early days, If I could leave everyone in the place rolling in the isles after I left it made me feel great also.

Each day I would go to three different businesses. I would try to stop by every business in my area at least once a week. It worked like magic. After I stopped by my three businesses for the morning, I finally made it to the bank and of course the same process would begin again. I tried not to get involved in lengthy conversations, because neither of us had the time. But I did try to have fun. When I would leave that bank, they knew I had been there. That enthusiasm works like magic and it's free to everyone. Have fun and you will win. If you focus on your problems, you will drown in them. Focus on the solutions to your problems and you will always win.

I saw this article in a local newspaper and I thought it was very interesting. "Word-of-mouth is a powerful tool in the world of business. Word-of-mouth is slow, but for those who have a great product, faith in that product and patience; word-of-mouth is the most effective way to build a business. My business was in that situation. Despite the fact that I advertised on four radio stations, advertised in the newspaper and even tried a little TV, it was word-of-mouth that built my business.

I've gone from 700 customers per week to over 1600 per week in only one year. All of this because one person tried our food. The next day, he brought a friend. The next day, his friend brought a friend and so on. Soon, we became a very successful restaurant with fifteen employees making a monthly payroll of $10,000. Word-of-mouth has been great for me."

I would say word-of-mouth is better than great, and you say, "Wait a minute; I've been open for years and I can't get my business to grow!" For word of mouth to work properly you must have a great product and have faith in that product. Investigate the quality of your food and the excitement of your crew.

Almost every small-town newspaper I've seen will do an article, complete with a picture, of any business of interest. Usually all you have to do is call and ask. I've used this method dozens of times. It's free to you because it's community interest. Each time I've had as article about one of my restaurants in the newspaper, the sales of the featured store would increase by 20%. If you're really prepared to dazzle these new customers generated by an article, you'll be able to maintain the increase. Try it. You'll be glad you did.

Advertising that's not free
Other methods of building sales are what I call the world of expense. This area is where you spend your hard-earned money advertising in newspapers, magazines, or television and radio. These methods are expensive areas for the independent, because

the independent normally does not have anyone with whom to share the cost.

It is difficult to monitor the results of advertising in the media. The independent normally cannot afford enough air time or the consistent newspaper coverage it takes to really see results. So, the key is to spend your money wisely. Be careful with advertising as you can spend your way to poverty in a hurry.

If you are financially sound enough to afford a strong advertising campaign, then have a goal. Make each of your spots very creative and different. Don't do the same old stuff. Create something everyone will want to see or hear again and again.

There's not much more I can tell you about the media which they can't tell you. I don't want you to think that I'm totally against advertising, because I'm not. I believe in value and results. Hard work has always worked better for me.

Keeping Excitement High

Keep the excitement flowing. Has the excitement level in your restaurant become stale? Excitement is just as important as the great food you sell. The level of excitement in your restaurant will bring customers to you. Your great food will have them coming back for more.

Always try to keep something new and exciting going on at your restaurant. Have your local high school have a car wash on your parking lot to raise money for the school. Let the high school cheerleaders be your waitresses for a day (with their uniforms on). They can work for tips for the school.

Rent a costume and put a great personality in it and put the person out by the highway.

Introduce a new and different menu item and heavily promote it.

Paint your building a different color.

A national restaurant chain, I use to work with, would have the entire crew go outside and run around the building. Now, can you imagine how this would loosen up the crew? Can you imagine what this would do to improve their attitudes? I understand how silly this seems, but it does work.

I hope you take several trips through this section because sales are usually at the root of all independent's problems. Having fun with what you are doing is always connected to your success. Don't be a slave to your restaurant.

Excitement begins with you. Your crew will be a reflection of you, just as surely as your children are a reflection of you. Get up from that chair and get excited about something.

EXCITEMENT GENERATES INTEREST
INTEREST GENERATES MONEY
MONEY GENERATES EXCITEMENT

Sales Decrease

We don't like to talk about a sales decrease in the restaurant business, however, it does happen. What are some of the things that can cause your sales to decrease?

#1 Attitude. One employee with a bad attitude can ruin your business. It makes no difference whether they have customer contact or not. A cook with a bad attitude can and will produce a bad product. That is not what your customers expect from you.

One crew member with a bad attitude can also ruin your entire crew. You must take action immediately to stop this attitude from spreading. This action will also send a message to your entire crew that a bad attitude will never be tolerated.

#2 Changing the quality of your food. You can never buy the best product and you can never pay the lowest price. There will always be something out there which is bigger, better and faster. You must, however, find a product you want to sell and stick with it. If you change from one brand to another, your customers WILL notice the change. That is dangerous.

When I was younger, I was the manager of a national fast-food restaurant. It was the first restaurant that I had ever managed. When this restaurant opened it was the highest volume restaurant in the chain. We were using a lower-quality but good tasting chili at this restaurant. After several months I decided I would thank my customers for their loyalty by upgrading the quality of the chili. The new chili was definitely a higher quality and it also had a higher price.

I was very proud to do this for my customers until I noticed that my chili sales had begun to drop. Even though the new chili was a higher-quality product, my customers were conditioned for the taste of the lower-quality chili. I learned my lesson then and there. Don't tamper with things that work.

#3 Time of year. A restaurant's sales will normally decrease after Christmas and remain low until late March. This has a lot to do with Christmas spending, winter, tax time, etc.

During this period of time, you must trim your crew back and watch your pennies closely. I call it, tucking away for the winter. This does not need to be a negative time for you. Around the end of March your sales will have that spring increase. You must spend these winter months planning for the spring increase. Knowing when to increase your crew again must be planned very carefully. If you add crew too late you will provide inadequate service to your customers. If you add crew too early, you'll have high labor costs.

Use these winter months to regroup. Plan some spring activities for your restaurant. Learn to capture your share of the spring boom and if you're able to capture more that your share, they will normally stay with you for the remainder of the year. Don't just let these spring increases happen. Get involved to make your spring increases better than usual. Set goals and reach those goals.

The month before school lets out can be a slower period of time for your restaurant. There are proms, graduation, vacation planning, softball and so many things going on in town to take attention away from you. Try to get involved with these activities. Sponsor a softball team. Stay active during this period of time and keep your restaurant visible.

#4 New competition. A new restaurant in town should not be a negative thing for you. It's actually healthy for you and everyone. A new restaurant will cause you to take a closer look at yourself and your operation. It's too bad that many independents wait for a new restaurant to open before they begin this self-examination.

If you're taking care of business with great food and enthusiastic service, then a new restaurant will normally only hurt you for a couple of weeks. Use this time wisely. Keep yourself busy. Maybe your building needs a paint job or a good cleaning. Do those things you've been meaning to do for a long time, but have just been too busy to do.

All the specials in the world won't help. Everyone is going to try this new place out and then come back home to you. If your service has been strong and the quality of your food has been exceptional, as I've been speaking of throughout this book, then your customers will be back. If it has not, you're in big trouble and you've got to upgrade the quality of your food and inject some excitement into your crew and you've got to do it NOW!

#5 Your first year. As an independent your first year will be full of ups and downs. Every time you experience a down in sales, investigate your service and the quality of your food. Keeping a record each day of anything, which may have an effect on your sales, will make you a better planner next year.

Factors that affect sales are:
Home football games
Easter
Thunderstorms
Prom
Graduation
Oktoberfest
Parade

The first year you're on your own. Next year you will know what effect each of these will have on your sales. Carefully record each and every event for next year. This will be very helpful to you next year when planning labor for a particular day, week or month.

#6 The economy. During my forty years in this business, I've heard many people, from time to time say, "Sales are down because of the economy." The only problem with that statement is that I have never personally experienced a decrease in sales because of the economy. Not once. I believe the economy is just an easy thing on which to blame low sales.

There are exceptions of course. If your local economy depends on a major factory and the plant closes, it could have a major effect on your sales. If this country were to experience a depression, it would definitely have an effect. "When the going gets tough, the tough get going." Ever hear that statement? It's true. If your sales become sluggish for any reason, don't blame it on the economy and throw in the towel, roll up those sleeves and get to work. Use some of the sales-building ideas in this book. Get on the telephone and make those telephone calls today! Remind your customers of your monthly special. You and your customers will be glad you did. A weak economy is no reason to give up. People still eat. With a little prompting from you, they may eat at your restaurant.

Final Comments

As you can see, operating a restaurant is a very involved process. I would suggest that you work in the type of restaurant you wish to open for several months before you attempt to open your own place.

In the restaurant business, "KNOWLEDGE IS KING". The more you know the better your chances to find success.

If the coach of the Dallas Cowboys were to call you tomorrow and ask you to be his quarterback next year, you'd probably think he was crazy, and he would be. Because you don't have the training, knowledge or skill to quarterback the Dallas Cowboys.

People open restaurants every day with no more knowledge ofthe food business. Isn't that strange?

Sometimes, it's easy to confuse their kitchen at home with a kitchen in a restaurant. In other words, they feel if they can cook at home that they are qualified to open a restaurant.

They couldn't be farther from the truth.

The restaurant business is a people business. Learn to deal with people. Most independents will say, "Everybody likes me."

Learning how to deal with people has nothing to do with how many people like you. This is a business striving to make a profit, not a popularity contest. While you must be likable, you must also have the ability to achieve. This means directing your crew in a way, which is profitable for you and also pleasant for them. It means training your salespeople to give you the best product at the very lowest price possible. It means giving your customers the portions, which will satisfy their needs and at the same time be profitable for you.

Sometimes how you sell your product is far more important than the product you sell. Enthusiasm can sell almost anything if applied properly and enthusiasm is free to everyone.

A smile and excitement will attract people just as a light bulb attracts bugs at night. On the most part, your customers may have had a rough day with many problems. If so, it's a joy for them to go to a restaurant which is happy and full of excitement. One which is carefree but professional. One which is proud to have them as a customer and appreciates the fact that this customer chose to eat at your restaurant.

Learn to brainstorm to solve problems. If you have a problem in your operation, learn to search for all possible solutions. There is always a solution for every problem. Often times there are many solutions.

Being organized in this business is critical. This business is so fast moving and complex that you simply must be organized to survive. Daily organizers and monthly bill organizers are great tools to help you stay organized. Any forms you may design to help you stay organized would be a step in the right direction.

Do not put things off, as they will pile up on you quickly. Dealing with problems as they arise is and has always been the best policy for you to operate by. Never put off till tomorrow what you can do today. This will keep you from being overwhelmed with problems and maximize your profits.

To my knowledge, there has never been help available for the independent restaurant owner. I hope that in some small way, that I've been able to help you better understand this complex and difficult business that we share.

The next time you hear someone say, "Honey, you make the best chili, we should open a restaurant and sell it," I expect you to jump to their rescue.

HAVE A GREAT CAREER!

How to Open a Re$taurant and Keep it Open
Book and Audio Series

In 1962, Tom Bradburn began his restaurant career as a carhop at an independent fast-food restaurant. Three years later, he landed a job with a national fast-food chain. For almost a decade, Tom learned the restaurant business, working his way up to manager and part-owner. For two of those years, his restaurant, set national sales and profit records.

From 1972 until 1982, Tommy acquired several of those existing chain restaurants which, were in trouble and he also opened a few new restaurants. By developing training manuals and working on training films, as well as creating a training school for managers, Tom was able to teach many students the finer points of restaurant management.

A decade ago, Tommy's tastes turned to independent restaurants and opened several of his own gourmet burger operations. He quickly realized that the independent restaurant owner is often without the training necessary to be successful in this highly competitive business. Thus, he created a successful consulting business catering to independent restaurants. From this nucleus of experience and training, Tommy Bradburn has created both the book and 4 MP3 audio series designed specifically for those in the business or those considering opening their own restaurant.

The book and MP3 audio series designed specifically for (and dedicated to) the independent restaurant owners of America.

MP3 files are three hours of critical and motivational material. $19.95. The best $20 you will ever spend

Other services offered by The Restaurant Consultant

On sight Restaurant evaluations

Multi-Unit Management Workshops

Multi-Unit Employee Seminars

Multi-Unit Motivational Seminars

Business Plan for your Restaurant

The Restaurant Consultant
Tom C. Bradburn
575-587-0502
tcbradburn7@gmail.com

If you are interested in the 4 MP3 audio files, drop me an email